MY NAME IS

IZZY

*To Celia and Jim
with gratitude and love
from Izzy*

IZZY COVALT

Strawberry Hill Press

Strawberry Hill Press
3848 S.E. Division Street
Portland, Oregon 97202-1641

Cover by Ku, Fu-sheng
Edited by Kristi Burke
Typeset and design by Lee G. Spratt, Mosier, Oregon

Manufactured in the United States of America

Library of Congress Cataloging-in-Publication Data

Covalt, Izzy J., 1927-
    My name is Izzy / Izzy J. Covalt.
          p.   cm..
    ISBN 0-89407-128-9 (trade paper : alk. paper)
    1. Covalt, Izzy J., 1927-   . 2. Restaurateurs—Oregon Biography.
3. Women alcoholics—Oregon Biography. 4. Women alcoholics—Rehabilitation—Oregon Biography. 5. Oregon Biography. I. Title.
CT275.C8538A3   1999
305.4'092—dc21
[B]   99-24091
                                                           CIP

Behind her tidy desk, my interviewer looked professional and in control. She spoke very softly, but directly. This was an unusual position for me to be in. Usually I was the one conducting the interview. I'd been asking my employees questions for twenty-two years, since 1959, and I wasn't accustomed to being questioned.

As I lay on the bench outside the nursing station that afternoon, waves of nausea overwhelmed me. My limbs trembled uncontrollably. That shaking, however, was nothing compared to the shaking that consumed me internally. The feeling was familiar. I had tried to go without alcohol at home the previous weekend, but I hadn't let the withdrawal progress this far. I feared for my life.

Bunny stayed with me as long as the nurses would allow that first night at Serenity Lane. This was so different than how I had imagined her visit. Her call to tell me she was coming had been an appalling development for me. But she insisted. She said our brother Fred would be coming, too. I didn't understand why she would choose to come at that time. Bunny was teaching and no school vacations were scheduled. It would mean hiring a substitute teacher. And why Fred? Their visit would interfere with my drinking.

I applied and was accepted into the Army Cadet Nurse Corps shortly before the end of World War II. I attended classes at Providence School of Nursing in Everett, Washington, only seventy miles from home. Because the war created a need for nurses, the government paid full tuition, room and board, and books for all students in this program. It was marvelous for less fortunate women who otherwise might not have had the opportunity to go beyond high school. My financial position was stronger than most, but it was a great help to have all expenses paid. We also received a monthly fifteen-dollar stipend.

The attacks increased in intensity and frequency. I sometimes needed to leave the office or get up from a luncheon meeting to walk around the block to bring my breathing back under control. And on more than one occasion I was so frightened, I asked Jim to take me to the emergency room. I went to my internist, who prescribed librium, and to Dr. Kimball, who increased my dosage of valium. Afraid to risk having my tranquilizer dosage reduced, I didn't tell either doctor about the other's prescriptions.

Recovery, for me, is the joy and the awareness that I am again a valuable human being with a purpose for living. It is through serving God as I understand him that I believe I can attain and feel that sense of purpose in my life. I can support my family, friends, employees, and other recovering alcoholics on their individual paths. I also believe it is my duty to reach beyond those who are close to me and contribute to the community.

Izzy on Buster, 1931.

Dedicated to ——
Mom and Daddy.

Izzy at about three years old, 1930.

Acknowledgments

The support of many to keep writing meant everything to me. Their ongoing enthusiasm and interest made it easier to keep working.

I knew I had a story to tell—about family, about women as leaders, about business, and about alcoholism and recovery.

I first told friends Jack L. and Jeanette T. in 1990 that I intended to write my autobiography. They believed in my story, and I began to write.

All of my copious and sometimes almost illegible handwriting was put on the computer by a trusted former employee, Janet Silver, who made herself available for a quick turnaround despite her full-time job. My trust in her gave me the courage to put down on paper my sometimes painful memories.

My friend Joyce Greiner painstakingly reviewed and edited over the period of years that I labored on the first draft. She, especially, never stopped believing that I had an important story to tell to women, and she lovingly pressed me on. I will forever be indebted to her.

Each of my children questioned, critiqued, and encouraged. My sister Bunny helped me with some of the historical material. Granddaughters Ashley, Heather, and Courtney both cried and laughed as they listened to me read the story aloud. They were wonderful sounding boards—especially Ashley, who was only ten years old when it all began.

I had so wanted Cousin Carlie, my best friend as a little girl, to see my book published and to read it. I never got to share it with him. He died of lung disease September 20, 1998.

Daughters-in-law Jeanie Covalt and Elizabeth Covalt have shown extreme interest and excitement when they inquired about my progress. Son-in-law Frank Imhof has done some critiquing and has been somewhat impatient with the length of the process—but has always been interested and encouraging.

Author Charlie Stoakes spent many hours editing, advising, and rewriting. Thank you, Charlie, for your assistance and your continuing inspiration.

Throughout my writing I shared parts of the manuscript with

Kathleen M., Betty C., Kathleen P., Susan M., and Linda R., who are all women in recovery. They became part of my cheering squad. I desperately needed their approval and support, and I received both throughout.

Others who showed love and interest were friends Dorothy Pollard, Frank and Kitty Fisher, Veronica Morgali, Myrna Visser, Deb Lacey, Jan Schmeltzer, and other women in recovery: Rhoda M., Georgia D., Earline B., Patty M., Sue S., and Kim S.

After Joyce Greiner helped revise and proofread yet another time, Jan Lowen took the discs that Janet Silver had worked on. Jan put the manuscript on fresh discs. Vail did a final proofread. I was now ready to search for a publisher.

The search began. I received input from Vail, Joyce, Charlie, and daughter Patti, who all had some familiarity with publishing. I, of course, had none. Jan Lowen helped with correspondence, and Trish House helped by researching the library for publishers who we thought might be appropriate.

Thank you, Dr. Jean-Louis Brindamour of Strawberry Hill Press, for responding with interest and for suggesting Kristi Burke for still more editing and revision. It was a joyful time—that time spent with Kristi. We met at Izzy's Restaurants many mornings. Thank you, staff at Izzy's Gateway, Izzy's Clackamas, Izzy's Eastport, Izzy's Keizer, Izzy's Lancaster in Salem, and Izzy's South Commercial in Salem. We were always warmly welcomed, made comfortable, and fed well. Kristi helped me with the difficult task of eliminating some of the stories, many of which included people who are dear to me.

And then Jean-Louis gave the go-ahead. He was ready for Strawberry Hill to publish.

Thank you—each and every one—and now I can only pray that what I have written will make a difference.

Izzy Covalt

Chapter 1

Behind her tidy desk, my interviewer looked professional and in control. She spoke very softly, but directly. This was an unusual position for me to be in. Usually I was the one conducting the interview. I'd been asking my employees questions for twenty-two years, since 1959, and I wasn't accustomed to being questioned.

She asked me where I had come from and whether I had driven myself. The two beers I drank on my way there, along with the two tranquilizers, were working quite well, and I felt good about how I had pulled myself together that morning. I was wearing one of my favorite silk blouses, my wool tweed skirt, gold jewelry, and heels.

"It's a good thing I wore this tweed skirt," I thought, as I felt my bladder release, "because the dampness won't show."

Often there was no longer an urge or warning when my bladder needed emptying. It just happened. A nurse took me upstairs where I exchanged my moist clothing for pajamas and a robe. I experienced a momentary concern when she took my purse, but resigned myself. I wouldn't need keys or identification for the next few days. Or would it be weeks? No one knew exactly.

I had hoped to hold on to the tranquilizers.

I was assigned a room next to the nurses' station called the "detox" room, where I was expected to stay until all the alcohol was out of my system. The dreaded withdrawal wasn't long in coming. As the familiar torture began I walked out of the room and into the hallway. I wanted to be where I could see someone. I found a bench near the nurses' station and huddled in a fetal position as withdrawal progressed.

Mom flashed into my mind. She always fixed toast in hot milk when I was sick as a child. I was relieved that she couldn't see me now. She would be so disappointed in me.

Then I thought about Daddy and I longed for him to hold me and call me "Baby" again as he had when I was a little girl. I loved to sit on his lap after supper before he went out to do the evening milking. His cheeks were whiskery, and even though sometimes it felt too scratchy, I loved to brush my face against his cheek. He would smile and cuddle me, making a game of it. I adored him. His voice was always gentle. Patient.

Even with his horses, Molly and Bess, the big Belgians he used for the heavy farm work, he never raised his voice.

▼ ▲ ▼

Our farm was located in Ten Mile, Washington. Daddy and one of his brothers, Uncle Carl, bought the farm from Grandpa on contract after World War I. Uncle Carl moved into Grandpa's log house and they built "the little house" for Daddy about a quarter mile away. The big old barn sat between the two houses and the farm was run as a partnership in every way.

One of my first childhood memories was around plowing with Daddy. It was the work I liked best. It was more like play. Daddy's priorities were typical of most farmers of his time. Some mornings he would give me a choice between helping him or going to school. Mom didn't encourage this, but usually didn't interfere, and so I would stay home to keep him company if he was going to plow. I felt as though I was helping him as I followed him through the fresh furrows and listened as he spoke gently to his horses.

I loved it when he let me ride Molly. But my favorite horse was a wonderful Shetland pony named Buster. I was four when Buster came into my life in 1931. Daddy introduced me to him at Earl Hickey's farm where I watched jealously as Earl's kids rode him. I was surprised and delighted a few days later when Mr. Hickey delivered Buster to our farm.

I had no fear the first time I rode Buster. He trotted off across the field with me hanging onto his mane and I slid off when he stopped abruptly at the fence. Unhurt, I chased him back to the barn where the men were standing and asked Daddy to help me get back on. That must have settled something for him because he complimented me on my riding and Buster stayed.

Between the two families there were seven kids on the farm at the time we got Buster and we all enjoyed him. But there was something special about Buster that made him seem like only mine. I helped feed, water, and brush him. Later I learned to harness Buster, hitch him to his cart and drive him up and down the lane. My parents often commented on what a great job I did of taking care of him and they were proud of the way I rode him and drove him on the cart. I loved the freedom of being outside where I also could climb trees, bounce in the hay, and play games with my cousins. We laughed and played freely outdoors.

Inside, at my house, it was different. Our "little" house was an extremely clean and tidy place. We had electricity, but no indoor plumbing until I was seven. Even without running water, Mom kept a spotless house. Never in a bathrobe, she was already well-groomed and neatly pressed by the time she served breakfast at 7:30 a.m.

She had a regular schedule for all housework. The washing was done on Monday mornings, the ironing done on Tuesday. Even wiping the chair rungs and rubbing down the stairway on hands and knees had a specific place in the Saturday morning schedule. I was seldom able to perform household chores up to Mom's expectations. The corners were never clean enough, my shoes were never shiny enough.

I loved my visits to the "other" house. Exciting things seemed to happen there. We could play indoors and make noise and messes. We could even snack between meals. We spent Christmas and other holidays there because it was larger.

When I was five, my six-year-old cousin Carlie and I decided I should move to the other house. Everyone said it would be all right so I gathered all my possessions into a drawer and we lugged the drawer over to Carlie's house and put it in a corner of his room.

When I sat down to eat with them that day, Uncle Carl reminded me that he already had several children. "I won't be able to afford any new clothes for you," he said, "but your Aunt Irene can make over my old underwear for you when it's worn out." I got to thinking about Uncle Carl's underwear and moved back home that afternoon.

A week or so later I watched as Uncle Carl and his family left to visit Aunt Molly and Uncle Leonard in Chillawack, Canada. Chillawack was one of my favorite spots. "What a fool I'd been," I thought. "I could have gone with them if I hadn't been so particular about Uncle Carl's old underwear."

As time went by, I began to realize that there were advantages to Mom's energy and discipline. Because her work was always finished early, we had free time every afternoon. We visited someone nearly every day until I started school. She would carefully prepare Daddy's lunch before we left and leave it on the table under a neat white cloth.

"Where are we going today, Mama?" I would ask.

We frequently went to the chapel for Johelo Club meetings. Johelo was a service club made up of most of the women in the community. They brought all of the kids with them who weren't in school and this is where I met and played with nearly everyone close to my age. Mom's Johelo Club often made and raffled quilts and crafts to raise money for community projects.

Other times we would go to visit friends. In a social setting, Mom was relaxed and fun. She was generous and was a dependable leader. One of Daddy's comments was that she was always the prettiest woman in a group. I thought so, too.

Four- and five-year-olds were sometimes allowed to visit the two room Ten Mile school and Mom often dropped me off there. I would receive a report card marked excellent and could seem to do no wrong. Bunny and some of my cousins were there and I loved running from room to room and getting lots of attention. It was like an unofficial nineteen thirties version of Headstart.

All of these experiences made me aware that many people approached life differently than Mom. Other people seemed more relaxed, seemed to have more fun and freedom. Mom rarely seemed comfortable with that. She had certain standards for behavior. People should be ambitious, clean, polite, and have high morals.

Mom had been raised in the strict discipline of the Nazarene church. She left the church when she married Daddy. Although she didn't officially become a Lutheran until after I was out of high school, she raised her children as Lutherans. As a member of the Lutheran community in Ten Mile, she could now enjoy card playing, dancing, and movies. She never came to tolerate smoking or alcohol.

Mom wasn't born in Ten Mile. Her family came to Ten Mile from Alberta, Canada, when she was ten. They were very poor. Her dad sold the produce he raised on a small plot and later sold eggs door-to-door. He was a strict father, always in a dress shirt and tie. Grandma was sweet and gentle and at all times trying to please him.

When Mom was thirteen, despite her dreams of going to high school, she was expected to go out and earn a living. She got a job as a live-in housekeeper and sent her paycheck home to her dad, who used it to support the rest of the family. Mom very much wanted to use some of the money to send her little sister, Essie, to high school. But her dad would have none of it.

One of Mom's jobs was for Joe and Hannah Myers, who had four children. This was where Daddy, a neighbor of theirs, first noticed her. Fifteen at the time, 4' 11", black sparkling eyes, black hair and olive skin, she was as cute as a button. She was nine years younger than Daddy. He made up his mind then that he would wait for her to be old enough to marry.

When she was sixteen, he entered the service and wrote her faithfully. They began dating when he was discharged a year later. They married on November 11, 1920, Armistice Day. She was nineteen. Daddy was happy to take her away from her hard life and had the little house on the farm ready for her to move into. Many times, I heard him say to her in a loving voice, "You'll never have to go back to taking care of someone else's home, will you Nell?"

Even though she no longer worked for the Myers, the children remained close to Mom and often visited her and Daddy at the farm. After their parents died, when the oldest girl, Louise, was fifteen, Mom became even more important in their lives. Louise and her younger sisters and brother ran the farm on their own. When they were sick or feeling low, they sometimes came to Mom for comfort.

Mom always felt strongly that she wanted to "give Daddy a son." But their first child was a girl, Bernita May, born May 7, 1923. Daddy immediately shortened her name to Bunny. They still wanted a boy when I arrived four years later, on April 23, 1927.

Mom enjoyed having a daughter like Bunny. She began teaching her homemaking skills. Bunny was quick to learn and mold herself after Mom. It was easy for me to see that Bunny was accomplishing and enjoying many of the same tasks as our mother did. Even snipping beans for canning appeared to be fun for them.

Bunny seemed to thrive in the house with Mom. I, on the other hand, found being in the house and working within the strict confines and high standards imposed there to be suffocating. I couldn't wait to get out the door. Bunny didn't give me a lot of attention, as we didn't cross paths too often. I always thought that I was a chore for her, but she sometimes attempted to have me assist her with whatever job she might be doing, usually without much success.

When Bunny was old enough to help Daddy in the barn she did it reluctantly. She did what she was told, but she didn't seem to enjoy it. I always responded to Daddy's requests and interests with an eagerness that pleased him. One of my favorite jobs with Daddy was plowing in the peat land, which was a low section of the farm where wood seemed to continually float to the surface.

We spent much of our free time gathering this wood with the horsedrawn sled and stacking it for burning. It was quiet and peaceful in the peat land. We would work together silently for long periods, enjoying the land and the companionship.

By the time my brother, Freddy, was born I was well entrenched in the "Daddy mode" and I stayed there. I don't recall anyone preparing me for Freddy's arrival. I was six when Mom disappeared and Bunny simply told me she had gone to get a baby. When I asked her where babies came from, she said they grew in gardens, and I didn't believe her.

"I'm just teasing you, Isabel," she said. "It's growing in Mom's stomach." I believed this even less.

Freddy was born November 16th, 1933, in the same house I had been born in, Mrs. Bond's Maternity Home, in Bellingham. I went with Daddy the next day to see him. I stood on tiptoes to look into his crib. He seemed to be made mostly of blankets.

Baby Freddy moved into the crib in Mom and Daddy's bedroom so I now slept on the daybed with Bunny. The daybed was not very private, serving as a couch during the day in our combination kitchen, dining room, and living room. I'm sure Bunny didn't like me joining her, but I didn't mind at all. One of my favorite games was to purposely and repeatedly move my foot over the imaginary line that Bunny drew. She would push it back. Each time she did, I cried out, and each time Daddy came out of his room with "leave that baby alone." Daddy never caught on.

In my entire childhood, Daddy only spanked me twice. I remember the first time vividly. The humiliation cemented it in my memory. Daddy was burning brush and several of us were playing around the fire. I teased my cousin, Erna, about something until she cried, and I didn't stop teasing when Daddy told me to. He took a strap off the harness and spanked my legs in front of everyone. Daddy did almost anything to avoid punishing me, but he couldn't tolerate my tormenting Erna. The spanking shocked me, but I immediately understood his message. This was my first difficult lesson about being a six-year-old.

When school started, I was disturbed to find that first grade didn't resemble my previous visits to school at all. It was hard. My teacher was new to the community. We didn't know her and she didn't know us. I was expected to sit down and stay there, a decidedly new and unpleasant experience for me. Lee Rohwer started school at the same time I did. He didn't like it, went home, and waited until the following year to start.

The Rohwer kids seemed especially lucky. They could do what they wanted, eat when they wanted, and speak any time they wanted. Mom didn't approve of this behavior, but to me, their house seemed filled with a kind of agreeable chaos. They lived directly across the road from school and regularly ate cold cereal and white store-bought bread. We were doomed to home-baked whole wheat bread and hot cereal everyday at our house. I loved to visit the Rohwers.

I also loved to visit Mrs. Brown. She was a fat, red-faced woman who worked in the fields or barn most of the time. She was critical of her neighbors, saying derogatory things about them, but was always happy to see me and invited me into her house for cookies or candy. I knew she could be mean to other people, but we got along just fine, even though Daddy told me I was probably her only friend. She wore short, loose dresses with nothing on under them and Daddy thought she was crazy. Daddy seldom criticized anyone, and when he said these things about Mrs. Brown, it made me even more loyal to her. Her husband, Sam, seldom talked, but when he did she would reprimand him and tell him to shut up and get back to work.

I got to visit Mrs. Brown every week to buy eggs when we couldn't get enough from our own chickens. After school, I carried the pail the quarter mile to her farm and after a nice visit with Mrs. Brown, brought back the eggs. Buying eggs from Mrs. Brown inspired me to think about selling eggs myself when Mom gave me a duckling to raise the summer I was seven. I was delighted when it began laying eggs. I made a large "Duck Eggs For Sale" sign and put it at the end of our lane where it met the Central Road. I had high hopes, but had forgotten that all the neighbors raised ducks of their own. Central Road was not heavily traveled and few people were in the market for duck eggs during the depression. My first enterprise was a flop, but it didn't dampen my enthusiasm for business.

This is one way I spent my after school hours. Otherwise, I lived for riding Buster, playing outside, and working with Daddy. I was always in overalls. Of course we went to school, church, and family dinners in dress-up clothes, but as soon as I got home, I always changed. Grandma Hallman was uncomfortable about this informal attire on her girls, but dresses weren't practical for play or chores.

One particular occasion made me especially happy to wear a dress. It was my seventh birthday and I was having a party. Birthday parties were rare in my family, and this was my first. My cousins, Carlie and Erna, and a half dozen friends were there and I'll never forget the fun and excitement I shared with them. I'd never had a big group of kids at my house. We played outside the entire time and there were presents and cake and ice cream. I felt special.

Soon after my party, Daddy began work on our new house. With the addition of Freddy we really needed more room! Daddy hired a carpenter to do the construction, but he dug the basement himself. I thought he needed my help and rushed home from school each day to assist him. He made a small scoop for me, just like his big one. I hitched Buster to this scoop and helped until supper. Once the house was completed, Bunny and I had a bedroom and shared a big double bed.

When school started that fall, I was disappointed to learn that the higher grades had moved to Laurel School and that now we had only thirteen kids, grades one to four, in the entire Ten Mile school. To me, this meant fewer playmates and less fun.

But, third grade also brought what I thought would be a delightful change. Louise Myers, the oldest of the Myers children, was our new teacher. By this time she was in her early twenties and her brother, Howard, was old enough to handle the chores on the farm. I was surprised and excited when I arrived for the first day of school to find that she was my teacher.

"Hi, Louise," I greeted her happily.

"It's Miss Myers to you from now on, Izzy." It didn't sink in. I considered our relationship to be equal and assumed my knowing her so well gave me the authority to be her assistant. She warned me several times about leaving my seat or talking when I should be listening, but I assumed too much and kept repeating this behavior. One day Louise tied me to my seat and kept me there all day. I was terribly embarrassed.

Things got even worse. I also talked a lot in class. I seemed to have the answer to most things most of the time. Miss Myers repeatedly asked me to be quiet. One day she had had enough, and taped my mouth shut. That did it. My behavior improved from that day on.

We had an old pot belly stove at Ten Mile school. We would arrive, take off our coats, and gather around the stove to keep warm until time to take our seats. It was Miss Myer's job to get there early and build the fire. The stove did more than keep us warm. During morel mushroom season, we all went out into the stumpy, partially wooded area across the road and gathered pails of the mottled shriveled mushrooms. When we brought them in, Louise sauteed them in butter over the stove. Everyone paid close attention to ensure that they got their equal share of this delicacy.

Eating the mushrooms at school was a big step for me, because I was usually finicky about what I ate. This had been a problem for me from an early age. Mom expected us always to clean our plates, no matter what was on them. She remembered the days in Alberta when food was scarce and she couldn't understand finicky eaters. I tried to eat everything, but had trouble many times. "Come on, Baby," Daddy would whisper when I objected to something, "eat it, and Daddy will give you a nickel." So I tried to eat, but often gagged, unable to finish. Daddy still slipped me a nickel under the table.

Other than the mushrooms, I dreaded eating at school. Our mothers took turns bringing hot lunches to school on a weekly rotating basis. I had no problem eating when it was Mom's turn, or Aunt Irene's, but I would look suspiciously at some of the other mothers' offerings. I believed that store-bought food didn't have germs, but I simply couldn't face the unknown of other people's cooking. One day Louise found I wasn't eating. "I want you to finish that, Izzy."

"I can't."

"Perry Crandall's mother fixed it and she is just as clean and just as good a cook as your mother."

"I know, but..."

"Now finish it!" I struggled on, trying not to think about what I was eating, but I simply could not eat Perry Crandall's mother's food.

My best friends at school were Hanky Duim and Hughie Sooter. We were inseparable except when Hughie and Hanky got to do things I wasn't allowed to do, like walk home the long way through the woods. Hughie came from a poor family, was quiet and well behaved in school, and was a great baseball player. I sometimes went to his house to get eggs and looked forward to seeing him. I became concerned about Hughie's long hair one day. His mother cut all her boys' hair, but didn't get around to it very often. I knew I shouldn't, but I took Hughie to a closet in the back of the school and trimmed him good. Hughie didn't mind, nor did his mother, but I was in trouble with Louise again.

Despite my energy and enthusiasm, which always remained a challenge to her, there were a lot of things I did that Louise liked. She organized many extra activities for us and I joined in wholeheartedly. One of her pet projects was the baseball team. Hughie, Hanky, and I loved baseball, but others had to be drafted onto the team as there were only thirteen students in the entire school. Louise coached us and drove us to the away games at Victor, Greenwood and Forest Grove.

The summer following third grade, Mom sometimes kept me occupied by putting me in charge of Freddy. She was often busy cooking huge amounts of food for the haying or threshing crews. Freddy was almost two, and a big responsibility. Mom was potty training him, and my job was to see that he didn't wet his pants while she was busy. I was specifically told to keep him away from the pears in the orchard. I tried, but would get distracted, playing with Carlie and Erna. I would suddenly remember Freddy and would invariably find him with the remains of several half-eaten pears and, of course, wet pants. I knew Mom would hold me responsible so I would sit him in the sun, hoping he would dry out before she checked on us. It didn't work. She somehow always knew.

There were fruit or cookies always available on the kitchen counter at our house in case we got hungry, but eating from the cooler or cupboard between meals was not allowed. I came home from school one day when I was eight and climbed onto the forbidden counter. I rummaged about and knocked over a jar of syrup that managed to fall all the way to the floor. It broke and splattered everywhere. I mopped and scrubbed and thought I did a pretty good job until Mom got home. Her first words when she walked through the door were, "What did you spill?" I couldn't imagine how she had known, but had to confess I had been in the cupboard.

It was less of a mystery to me to understand how Bunny knew I'd been wearing her best wool sweater. She hadn't given me permission to wear it to school and I wanted to be sure to return it to her in top condition. So I washed it, carefully, in hot water. It turned into a matted mess that brought Bunny to tears. I felt terrible. It bothered me for years and I looked for ways to make it up to her.

My relationship with Miss Myers improved by the time I was in fourth grade. It took me longer than the others to realize she was in charge, but I finally accepted it. My new attitude resulted in her encouraging me to help the younger children and I found myself happily involved as her assistant at last.

About this time, someone left Buster's gate open and he got out of his pasture and into a field of green oats. Nobody discovered this for some time and by then it was too late. Buster had over-eaten and his intestines were blocked. Daddy called the vet, but there wasn't anything he could do.

It was a warm, beautiful day and Buster lay on his side under a tree. I lay there with him until late that night. I can remember the family going in to supper. They let me stay. I alternated between sobbing and trying to talk Buster into getting well. I couldn't bear the thought of him dying, but Daddy said there was no hope, and I believed him. I prayed throughout the evening, pleading with God to cure Buster. When I wasn't praying, I cried.

Finally, after dark, Daddy came and coaxed me inside. I lay in bed that night, knowing Buster was out there alone, under the tree, dying. I jumped out of bed the next morning and ran to check on him, but he was gone. Daddy had removed his body. I didn't think I would ever feel worse.

Ten Mile School, 1936. Front Row (left to right) Hanky Duim, Keith Medcalf, Lee Rohwer, Dickie Rohwer, Hughie Sooter. Back Row: Teacher Louise Myers, cousin Erna Muenscher, June La Bounty, Isabel (Izzy) Muenscher, Frieda Miller, Emma Snowden, Luella Snowden.

Chapter 2

As I lay on the bench outside the nursing station that afternoon, waves of nausea overwhelmed me. My limbs trembled uncontrollably. That shaking, however, was nothing compared to the shaking that consumed me internally. The feeling was familiar. I had tried to go without alcohol at home the previous weekend, but I hadn't let the withdrawal progress this far. I feared for my life.

The nurses gave me small does of librium, but it wasn't enough to help. I asked repeatedly for more medicine. Didn't the nurses understand how badly my body needed help getting through this?

I waited anxiously for Bunny to arrive from Montana. She had already planned to visit. In the blur of the past few days I had forgotten about her coming, until suddenly, in the car on the way here, I had remembered.

"Your Aunt Bunny is coming today," I told my sons, Fred and Jim. "You must call and tell her what's happening before she leaves."

"She'll meet you at the treatment center this afternoon, Mom," Fred said softly. "We called her. She knows all about it."

I was touched. My faithful sister was going to be there to support me when I needed her most. When she finally arrived, I was too sick to show her how relieved I was. I had felt that Bunny's presence would bring me some kind of peace. And it did.

"Do Mom and Daddy know I'm here?" I asked Bunny, knowing full well what her answer would be.

"Oh, no," she said, "We can never tell them."

▼ ▲ ▼

I learned early that pleasing one's parents was important.

"Please, Nell, don't tell Ma," I remember Daddy pleading with Mom. I was seven or eight years old. Daddy had come in late. His speech was slurred and Mom was angrier than I had ever heard her before. She called him a drunk.

"Fritz Muenscher, I'm going to tell your mother," she threatened loudly.

"Don't tell her. I'll never do it again." This was the first time I saw Daddy drunk. I don't think he drank again until after his mother died.

Grandma Muenscher was a quiet, gentle woman, who spoke with a heavy German accent. Grandpa, who was outgoing, but strict, idolized her. His adoration for her was nearly matched by that of their three sons who remained close to both of them throughout their lives.

Grandpa and Grandma were delighted that Uncle Carl and Daddy had purchased their original farm. The families were linked not only by their ties to Grandpa and Grandma, but because Aunt Irene, Uncle Carl's wife, was Mom's sister.

Mom and Aunt Irene both had an especially deep regard for Grandma Muenscher. They admired the quiet way she commanded the respect of her husband and sons. Grandma was always there to offer counsel to those who needed her. Mom and Aunt Irene took turns making weekly visits to Grandma's to clean her house, wash her hair, and bring her laundry home to wash. It never bothered Mom that Grandma was not a great housekeeper, and she never begrudged the work she did for her.

Uncle Carl and Aunt Irene had six children. My cousin, Louise, was four years older than Bunny. Then there were Eleanor, Margie, Carlie, Erna, and Bobbie. I was between Carlie and Erna in age. They were my constant playmates. One family or the other visited Grandpa and Grandma each day. One of my favorite treats was an overnight stay with Grandma. I looked forward to my turn. Grandma made me feel so special when she tucked me into her fluffy feather bed. Although I was always finicky about eating away from home, this didn't apply to Grandma's house. I liked most of Grandma's cooking. Grandpa Muenscher always spoke proudly of it. I especially liked her creamed spinach fresh from the garden and her raspberries and cream. I sometimes found a live bug in the raspberries, but it didn't matter to me. Her home-baked rye bread was a delicacy, too. I loved my warm grandma, her simple foods and her equally simple, quiet life.

I also loved to go visit Mom's younger sister, Aunt Essie. She was married to Uncle Vernon and lived in Bellingham. Uncle Vernon was a carpenter. They had four sons, and because I was a girl I got special treatment. Aunt Essie had always wanted a girl, and I knew that she loved me as if I were her own. I followed her around the house as she worked. I felt I could say anything to her and was relaxed and happy when I was with her. Even cooking, cleaning, and painting seemed fun to Aunt Essie.

It was such a special treat for me when I was allowed to go visit her, but that didn't happen often. Instead, Aunt Essie often came to our house and pitched in and helped Mom with whatever project was underway, whether it was canning green beans, cooking for the threshing crew, or painting the kitchen.

She always made things fun, and Mom was more fun, too, when Aunt Essie was there. When Aunt Essie left after a day of work, her four boys in tow, Mom made sure that she took a box of fresh fruit or some of the fruits or vegetables they had canned that day.

Money was tight for Aunt Essie and Uncle Vernon and there was never a lot of extra food. Still, Aunt Essie's meals were abundant and tasted good, and she always saw to it that I had seconds if I wanted.

Dale, their oldest boy, was about six months older than I and we liked to play together. The boys all made me feel like a princess. I went trick-or-treating with them one year and it was exciting to have so many doors to knock on. Trick-or-treating on the farm consisted of carrying our lanterns to Uncle Carl's, collecting some candy, and returning home in time to answer Carlie and Erna's knock on our door. Every Halloween after that, I felt envious when I thought of my cousins gathering all those treats in Bellingham. But I never got to go again.

The year I finished fourth grade, they closed Ten Mile School and began construction on a new consolidated school at the same location. Most families opposed the new consolidation, but it went through anyway. This meant that we would attend Laurel School one year, which was a big change for all of us. We rode on a school bus and my class size increased from five to twenty-five. Enrollment at Ten Mile had been thirteen students; Laurel's was over two hundred. I liked it, and got good grades.

Though only a fifth grader, I was chosen to be the catcher on the girls' all-school softball team, mostly seventh and eighth graders. We got to travel, and I got a lot of praise, both at home and at school, for being such a good ball player.

I was involved in many activities in addition to the busy softball schedule. I joined 4-H, started piano lessons, and began having specific responsibilities at home, such as stacking wood and taking the slop to the pigs. Practicing the piano was one of the most time-consuming after-school activities. Mom had managed to save enough money to buy a piano that year. She dropped me off each Saturday afternoon for a lesson from a Miss Steed while she went shopping in Lynden. I enjoyed the lessons and liked piano, but didn't always practice. I would sometimes arrive unprepared and Miss Steed would reassign the same lesson for the following week. I disliked being unprepared and tried harder.

Of course I still missed Buster. I missed the freedom he had provided. Pestering Daddy for another horse seemed useless, as he refused to discuss the matter. But then, early in the school year, Babe showed up. She was an aged, stiff-legged bay mare that Daddy got somewhere. This helped some. At least I had a horse to ride. We only had her about a year before she disappeared. Because of her stiff legs, Daddy was afraid she'd fall if we ran her. He probably took her to Ruth's fox farm to be used for food, but I'll never know for sure.

With Babe gone, I began to badger Daddy for another horse. He wasn't responding, but I decided to earn some more money that I could put toward the horse for when he changed his mind. A friend of Daddy's, Fenton Myers, raised carrots commercially. I worked for him in my spare time, weeding. He paid me a dollar a day at first. This seemed like a fortune to me in those days and I saved most of it.

The summer following fifth grade was just as busy as the school year had been. I had fond memories of Laurel School, not the least of which was the day Benny Schessler kissed me on the cheek. I looked forward to the big new school at Ten Mile opening in the fall. I was sometimes allowed to work in the strawberry fields and I often spent entire days picking. Daddy would ask me how many pounds I had picked when I got home. He was interested in how much money I made and how I ranked among the other pickers. I was usually in the top two or three, depending on who was working that day, and he seemed pleased. I also worked in the bean fields when it didn't interfere with chores at home. I continued to do various jobs for Ruth Square and then weeded strawberries for the Boerhaves when Ruth sold out to them.

Daddy frequently emphasized the importance of being independent and preparing myself to work, not for someone else, but for myself. He often said, "You can earn big money working for someone else and then end up with nothing." He also encouraged me to save a portion of what I earned. Sometimes Daddy's attitude about money and about how the farm should be run seemed overly stringent to me. For him, it was a must to be prompt with the farm work and to be on a schedule. Play and time off came only when the jobs were complete. This meant sometimes missing a Fourth of July celebration or church on Sunday to get the hay in or to finish the threshing. These values have served me well, many times.

Hinote's Corner, pronounced "High-notes," was the central focal point in the area and the most prominent part of Ten Mile. It consisted of a little store with a gas pump, a garage, and the Grange building. All distances in Ten Mile seemed to be measured from the store. We lived south of "The Corner," as Daddy would say, about three-quarters-of-a-mile.

Mr. Hinote was always sitting when I came into the store, his feet propped on the old stove. I didn't want to bother him, so I waited on myself, recording my purchases on our family charge slip.

The Grange was one of the activity centers of Ten Mile. Dances were held there regularly on Saturday nights, but Mom wouldn't go because of the drinking that went on. I was told the men kept flasks of alcohol in their cars and spent as much time in the parking lot as they did on the dance floor. Friday night was different. Friday was "Grange Night," and Mom and Daddy often went. Sometimes they would take me along.

Our farm was located about halfway between the Grange and the other community focal point, Ten Mile Chapel. Sunday school and church were held there, as well as weddings, funerals, community meetings, and other activities. Almost every kid in Ten Mile attended Sunday school, even if their parents didn't go with them. Mom insisted that I go every Sunday. When I was little, I sometimes objected, but knew I had no choice. Eventually, I no longer needed Mom to remind me to get ready and my faith became so important to me that I attended on my own.

The summer I was eleven, Daddy received an emergency call from one of the neighbors. Grandma was very sick and we rushed to get there. Grandpa was crying when he met us at the door.

"Anna, my Anna," was all he could say, over and over.

It was the worst thing I had ever experienced. Grandma had had a stroke and Daddy was in agony. He loved her so. It seemed that life could never be the same again, and it wasn't.

It was difficult to find someone who would stay with Grandpa to help take care of Grandma. She remained physically strong, but the stroke changed her personality from a warm and loving woman to a person very difficult to manage. We tried many different arrangements with none being ideal.

Daddy often cried during Grandma's illness. I had never seen him cry before and it hurt to see him in such pain. Grandma suffered additional strokes and was finally bedridden. Grandpa set up her bed in their rarely used living room and used the large dining room for everything else.

Daddy frequently asked me to play "The Lily of the Valley" on the piano after Grandma's stroke. Sometimes as I played, I sang. Soon Mom's lovely alto voice joined from the kitchen where she'd continue working as we harmonized. "My bright and morning star the fairest of ten thousand to my soul." I tried not to cry as I watched Daddy wipe the tears from his eyes.

The night before Grandma died, she was in a semi-coma. To me, she looked asleep. Grandpa asked all the grandchildren to come in, one at a time, to say goodbye. We each took turns by her bedside, hugging and kissing her as we tried to talk to her.

After Grandma's funeral, Grandpa was lonely, and that summer I was the grandchild chosen to go live with him until he could find a housekeeper. It was something different, and fun. I was up at three-thirty each morning and out to the barn to help with the milking. I had been considered too young to do barn work before this, and the new responsibility felt good. It made me feel even more grown up when Grandpa began pouring fresh coffee for me each morning. This was my first experience with coffee and I enjoyed sharing it with him. After rye bread and coffee, I was off to the new school. I was in sixth grade. After school I would come home to Grandpa's and again help with the milking. Family visited each evening and I was in bed by seven or eight.

Grandpa had started a tradition of giving each of us grandchildren a calf when we reached the age of twelve. Mine was born about this time. I named her Lily, after Daddy's song. Later that fall, I returned home to my usual routine and took Lily with me.

When I was twelve I was still small, but solid from all my activities. My hair was pulled back in tight braids, which Mom braided for me every morning. I was covered with freckles everywhere. I seldom paid much attention to my appearance. Mom still bought my clothes and told me what to wear each day, and I didn't give any thought to my freckles until one day I was about to go out the door to school.

"How do I look, Mom?"

"You wouldn't look so bad," Freddy interrupted, "if you'd wash those spots off your face." Mom scolded him, but I took note.

Another time I came home with brand new saddle shoes and asked Bunny how they looked.

"Well…, they're nice looking, but they sure look like boats on you."

My feet were about the size they are today, and at twelve they were proportionately the biggest part of me. I was beginning to worry that I should pay more attention to my appearance, but I didn't know why. Was there something wrong with freckles? Besides, there was nothing I could do about my freckles or my feet, so I just went on about my business.

That year was special because Pastor Keller, the new Lutheran pastor at the Bellingham church, began holding afternoon services at Ten Mile Chapel. Prior to this, we had only had Sunday school at Ten Mile. I had often been asked to play the piano for Sunday school and this honor motivated me to practice. Now I occasionally played for the church service when the regular pianist couldn't come. I also began teaching pre-school Sunday school class. Mom and Daddy had been involved with the Bellingham church for special events, but now attended more often. I envied the kids whose fathers attended church with them every Sunday and often asked Daddy to come with me. Sometimes he said yes. I remember how proud I felt when he and I walked into church together.

The year I was in sixth grade was a hard year for me. I was the catcher for the girls' softball team again, but the fun and excitement of the previous year wasn't there. Again I was the youngest on the team, but didn't get the attention I had received in fifth grade.

The loss of Grandma and Daddy's continuing grief made things especially difficult. Daddy was even quieter than usual, although still kind and gentle. Frequently I would glance up at him at the table or in the barn and see quiet tears rolling down his face. This behavior frightened me. It continued for at least a year, and I worried that Daddy would never be happy again. Much of the time, I felt I was walking under a dark cloud that might never lift. Finally, in December, something happened to raise the family's spirits. My baby sister, Elinor, was born. She was quiet and good-natured and she was such a joy to both of my parents. She was my "precious sister." I loved to help take care of her. Until Elinor's birth, Daddy had always called me "Baby," never Izzy or Isabel. But then Elinor became "Baby" and I became "Efe," after a slow-moving fellow who lived in our community. I knew Daddy was teasing, but it hurt, nevertheless. Even so, I called Elinor "The Baby," just like the rest of the family.

The next summer Daddy and Uncle Carl divided the farm. They felt that should something happen to either of them it would be easier for their families if they held separate titles. We took the half without the barn and built a new one at a cost of two thousand dollars. Now I had a place for my own horse! I had saved all the money I had earned up to this point just for this purpose. Daddy contributed some more, and now I was ready to start looking.

It was pure pleasure and excitement, searching the countryside with Daddy for the right one. Mom occasionally came with us, too. We visited a ranch about six miles from the farm one Sunday and found a spirited pinto about sixteen hands. I knew he was for me as soon as I rode him. The rancher sold him to me for seventy-five dollars, including a saddle, and I rode him home. It was one of the greatest days of my life and I still have Champ's saddle hanging on a beam in the sunroom of my home.

I spent hours riding Champ and loved it, rain or shine. When I went after the cows, I went on Champ. He was my transportation and my safety. He was strong and big and I was fearless when I was on his back. I think Daddy felt the same way about Champ because he no longer restricted me to the farm. More freedom than ever!

This same summer, Daddy's older brother, Walter, came to visit. He and Aunt Minnie drove out from New York with their girls. Grandpa and the three brothers gathered everyone together for a picnic at our farm on the Fourth of July. Daddy decided to drop in at Fenton Myers' house early that morning to visit before the picnic. He didn't come home as the day progressed and I became concerned. Fenton didn't have a phone so Uncle Carl went to find him. Uncle Carl returned without Daddy and it was whispered about that Daddy was drunk.

I had seen a drunk in Ten Mile. He didn't work and went from one friend or relative to another asking for handouts. I began visualizing Daddy doing this. I felt terrible. The pleasure I felt at the family getting together for something other than a work party was ruined. I envied my cousins whose fathers didn't drink and who were able to enjoy the day.

I well remember the feelings of shame I felt as the picnic progressed and I tried not to make eye contact. My cousins talked in low tones about "Uncle Fritz and his drinking."

"If he wouldn't show up for a day as important as this, what else might he not show up for?" I thought.

I don't remember who the two men were who brought Daddy home that night, but I doubt he could have managed on his own. Mom talked to him about leaving and about divorce as she put him to bed. She said she wasn't going to put up with it again. I was afraid Daddy's drinking would get worse if Mom left him and I was terrified. Some of our relatives said it was Fenton's fault, but I didn't think so. Experience had shown that Daddy would drink if the alcohol was there, and I resolved to be with him as often as possible. Daddy couldn't handle it when he was by himself.

The 'new house' built in 1933 on the farm at Ten Mile, Washington.

The 'new barn' built in 1939.

Chapter 3

Bunny stayed with me as long as the nurses would allow that first night at Serenity Lane. This was so different than how I had imagined her visit. Her call to tell me she was coming had been an appalling development for me. But she insisted. She said our brother Fred would be coming, too. I didn't understand why she would choose to come at that time. Bunny was teaching and no school vacations were scheduled. It would mean hiring a substitute teacher. And why Fred? Their visit would interfere with my drinking.

My solution to the problem was to stock my bedroom closet with wine. I was confident I could keep from drinking until evening if I had to, and my plan was to excuse myself early and retire to the privacy of my bedroom. Now, instead of being home, alone in my bedroom, drinking myself into oblivion and avoiding Bunny, I was grateful to have her with me.

I was surrounded by strangers. Even though Bunny was a comfort, I felt overwhelmingly alone. As a girl I had felt connected to God. My faith had been a constant source of comfort and guidance. I had somehow relinquished that faith in favor of alcohol and now felt a vast, crushing emptiness inside me. I felt unworthy of anything, let alone God's grace.

As the evening approached, the activity in the hallway increased.

"Who are all these people, Bunny?"

"Those are other patients."

In my bleary-eyed condition, anyone who was dressed and walking around looked healthy. I said as much to Bunny.

"They are all at different stages of recovery," she explained. "But believe me, most of them don't look normal."

▼ ▲ ▼

From a young age, Bunny had always had an opinion about how people should be dressed and groomed. She had always been quick to comment on my looks. The summer before I started high school she had informed me that my braids would no longer do. I needed a haircut and a perm.

My frizzy new look was just one change in a year of many changes. Bunny was going off to college. I had watched her grow up under strict rules. She had been under more pressure to perform than I had been, probably because she was the oldest child. Mom expected her to excel in the same things her cousins did, which forced Bunny to be constantly comparing herself to others. This comparison wasn't easy for her and she was often anxious, but she was dependable and a good student.

She had fought for permission to wear makeup, to use the car, and to go on her first date. When she decided to go to college, a different kind of challenge arose. She wanted to go to Washington State, which meant travel and dormitory costs in addition to tuition and books. Money had to be found and set aside. I was aware of the struggle and wanted to help, but wasn't sure how to go about it.

I had gradually rebuilt my savings account after purchasing Champ and withdrew twenty dollars. I was embarrassed to give it to Bunny openly so I left the money in her room with a short note. She still talks about how much it meant to her when she found it, and I was proud to have been able to contribute.

Bunny's school tuition added to Daddy's burden at a time when the depression was still making finances difficult. Bunny helped by waiting tables part-time.

Before school started, we all went shopping in Bellingham. Pete Zuidmeer, whom Bunny was dating regularly, came along. We split up to do our errands and agreed to meet at the car at a certain time. The time arrived and we were all there except Daddy. Pete went looking for him. He finally found him in a tavern. Daddy had to be helped to the car and was apologetic, slurring his speech. It was unpleasant and humiliating. Mom drove home angrily.

Mom again threatened to leave Daddy for drinking, and I was beginning to fear he wouldn't be able to keep from drinking if she did. Over the next few days, I heard her chastise Daddy about his weakness for alcohol. He was quiet and apologetic and promised never to drink again.

Once more, things returned to normal, but the fear of what alcohol might do to Daddy was with me more than ever. I had worried about his drinking since the Fourth of July incident years before. If he were a little bit late or was away from home without me, I'd fear he might be drinking again.

Because of this fear, I had long insisted that I accompany him wherever he went. Sometimes he'd say "No, you're not coming." I'd answer, "Yes, I am." And I usually did. I don't believe he had any idea why I was so persistent. I'm sure he would have been sad and hurt had he known that I was so bothered. My vigilance increased after the Bellingham episode.

By this time, I was carrying nearly half the work load on the farm with Daddy. I got up at five-thirty, rode Champ bareback for the cows, and drove them to the barn for milking. Daddy met me, and the cows headed to their stanchions for grain. I kept the barn odor out of my hair by covering my head with a freshly washed flour or sugar sack during milking. We were milking about thirty head by hand each day, including my Lily, and I kept after Daddy to buy milking machines. Nearly all the dairymen had converted to machines by this time, but Daddy was reluctant to spend the money. I think he was mistrustful of all the innovative new equipment.

With the cows, calves, young stock, and horses, we had around a hundred head of stock. In the winter, I climbed into the mow twice a day to throw hay down for them.

By seven-thirty I was in the house where Mom had breakfast ready. We had fruit, hot cereal and eggs every day. In addition, we had pancakes, French toast or waffles, and bacon, ham or sausage. Mom seemed to know when we were on the way in, and the food would be freshly prepared and just ready as we came through the door.

I ate in a hurry, then washed and dressed for school. Then it was out the door to catch the school bus or a ride to Lynden with a friend of Daddy's who worked at Darigold. If I missed both rides, I had to run-walk all the five miles to school. I hated to be late.

As always, the school year was busy and exciting for me. I finished my year of confirmation classes at church and was confirmed into the Lutheran faith. I still taught Sunday school and played the piano for services whenever I was needed. The high school group met every week encouraging spiritual growth. We also had fun with our pie socials, hay rides, and caroling parties. And, of course, I was still active in sports which meant a five mile run-walk after practice to get home for the six o'clock milking.

Instead of going to Meridian High with my friends, I went to Lynden High. My parents, still upset about the school consolidation that had taken place over the past years, were adamant that I would go where Bunny had gone.

I didn't support my folks' decision at first, but I soon became excited about meeting new friends, the busy character of the school, and the challenge of the curriculum.

The first day of school got off to a great start when I walked into my "home room" and saw Al Jansen assigned to the seat across the aisle. I had met him a year earlier when my cousin Eleanor married his brother, Hank. Al was good-looking, with twinkling eyes and an infectious smile. I was smitten.

I already pictured myself as being a lot like Eleanor, and the idea of me marrying her husband's brother seemed fitting. Over the past year, I had already envisioned a wedding like Eleanor's, and thought of Al often, even though I seldom saw him.

Al still looked good to me when I walked into class that first day. I couldn't believe my good luck. He seemed happy to see me, too. We never said much more than "Hi" that year, but that was enough to keep me dreaming about him.

In December 1942, I was invited to a Christmas party. By this time, I was a sophomore. Al was also invited. It was exhilarating to think about being around him for a whole evening, but I was even more excited when he asked me to go to the party with him! This was the stuff dreams were made of, but first I had to get over the hurdle of asking Mom and Daddy. It wasn't easy, but Bunny was home at the time and came to my rescue. I remember the evening well, not because it was my first date, but because everything happened as I had hoped it would.

Al arrived driving his family's panel truck. It might as well have been a stretch limo. He did everything properly, came to the door for me, and was attentive all evening. It was a wonderful party and his sense of humor captivated me. I knew I was in love before it was over. From then on, we were a couple.

My cousin Eleanor seemed delighted about seeing Al and me together. She and I already had a lot in common, and my dating her husband's brother made the bond even closer. Eleanor's husband, Hank, drove a truck for a living and was seldom home when I visited. Al didn't attend school often, preferring to work for his dad in their family landscaping business.

By the time Al was seventeen, he no longer attended school at all. He went to work for Hank, driving one of the trucks Hank bought to begin the Lynden Transport Company. Al was eighth in a working family of twelve children. Few of them graduated from high school, but most of them went on to become successful business people. Even though Al was no longer in school, we continued to date.

When I was a junior in high school, a routine test showed that our entire herd was infected with Bangs disease. The news devastated Daddy. Every cow and calf would have to be destroyed. He seemed dazed and exhausted as he made the arrangements to have the herd picked up and taken to the slaughterhouse as soon as possible. A truckload at a time, we saw the herd disappear down the road. I couldn't watch as they loaded my Lily onto the truck. It was unbearable to think about what was going to happen to her at the end of that ride. I sobbed for hours. It all seemed like a bad dream.

Fortunately, Daddy was a good businessman and had funds available to rebuild the herd immediately. An inoculation for Bangs disease was developed a short time later, but it sadly came too late to save Lily and the rest.

At the lowest point of the depression the milk checks had been as little as seventy-five dollars a month. During the war, they soared to as much as fifteen hundred dollars. By the time Lily died, in 1943, Daddy was paying me thirty dollars a month for all the work I did on the farm and for Lily's milk. Even with the climbing milk prices he had held me to the thirty dollar agreement. When Lily died, though I never replaced her, I still got the same amount.

Because I wanted to earn more money, I badgered Daddy to let me work for other farmers in my spare time, and he let me. I picked strawberries and beans and did weeding and hoeing. Due to the war-time labor shortage and inflation, I was paid a dollar an hour for this work. I was occasionally hired along with one of Daddy's teams. This was a great opportunity for me. Kids were not usually hired to hay. At these jobs, I did a man's work, and was treated as an adult, even eating with the men.

Daddy went to a livestock sale one day and was brought home late in the afternoon by strangers. They helped him into the barn, and by the time I got there, he had passed out. I went ahead with the milking, hardly believing he had left all the work to me. It was the only time I had to do everything by myself. I stopped to see how he was from time to time and scolded him even though he was in a stupor.

Daddy believed so strongly in the importance of an established and regular milking schedule that nothing, even illness or extreme weather, would cause him to deviate from it even by half-an-hour. And here he was, lying in the hay, unable even to walk, while the cows needed milking. It terrified me that he would do this. This was not the dad I knew.

He was very apologetic the next day, asking me over and over to forgive him. I was determined that he know how disappointed I was.

"Don't touch me," I said, "don't come near me, you're nothing but a drunk and I can't trust you."

"Please, Baby," he replied, "don't talk to Daddy that way. I love you. I'm sorry. I won't do it again."

His calling me "Baby" touched me and brought tears to my eyes, even though I was so angry with him. He had seldom called me "Baby" since Elinor had arrived. Even so, I didn't soften immediately. It took a couple days for me to forgive him and for the tension to ease.

On my sixteenth birthday, some of my classmates, all girls, surprised me with a party. Unsuspecting, I came in from the barn to find them hiding everywhere in our living room. I was so shocked I could hardly breathe. This was the second time Mom had given me a real birthday party with friends attending and I hadn't expected it. We giggled and ate and talked about boys. It was such an exciting thing to have happen.

I had many girlfriends and I often had a friend over to spend the night. Aside from Joy, a friend whose farm was close to ours, I could never stay with them because I had to be home for the morning milking. My parents always welcomed my friends as long as I got my chores done.

The summer I was sixteen, Erna, two friends and I took a week-long trip by ourselves to Vancouver, British Columbia. We took the train. It was a big step for us and perhaps a bigger step for our parents. I was the oldest one there and I still marvel that they trusted us so far away from home. We were all hard workers with money to spend so we stayed in a beautiful hotel, took cabs everywhere, ate out, went to movies, visited Stanley Park, and shopped and shopped. Bunny came home to help Daddy while I was gone, something that required careful coordination. It was my time off for the year.

About this time Grandpa Muenscher died. He had lived for five years after Grandma's death. Since he wouldn't see a doctor, we never knew exactly what he died from, but everyone suspected cancer. He wasted away, unable to eat or swallow. At his request, he was still at home when he died. Because his illness didn't take us by surprise, as Grandma's stroke had, the family was much more peaceful about Grandpa's death, and it didn't cause the same upheaval.

Also in 1943, Al was inducted into the Army Air Corps. I went with him and his family to Seattle to put him on the train to California for basic training. I was in love and dreaded seeing him go. It was over a hundred miles back to Ten Mile, but I don't remember much about the trip because I was so upset. He came home several times during those first six months and we wrote each other nearly every day.

Al served as a gunner on a B-29 in the Pacific. He wrote frequently and I anxiously awaited his letters. I felt confident that he would return. Nevertheless, I read the newspapers and listened to the radio with anticipation and fear. The war was part of our daily life. Along with the rest of the country we experienced rationing and shortages. After Pearl Harbor, because we were so close to the coast, there also seemed a real threat of invasion. We had periodic blackouts in anticipation of possible bombing.

Although I didn't understand the significance of it until years later, the boy/girl ratio in my high school class was radically affected by the war. By the time I was a senior there were only about six boys in a class of forty. The rest of the boys were either off to war or deferred from the draft so they could work on their family farms. Because I had grown up under these circumstances, it all seemed normal to me. It didn't seem as though the war would ever really end.

When it was time to go to the annual Junior/Senior Banquet, which required both a date and a formal gown, I had neither. But I didn't want to miss it. I snooped around in Bunny's side of the closet and found one of her old formals. It was too big, but I just tucked it in and went by myself. I had a great time.

The fall of my senior year, an opportunity came to work in the potato fields for a week. The pay was especially good, and I took a week off from school to do it. Champ made potato picking possible, as there was no way I could use the family car. After morning milking I rode him ten miles to the potato fields. He grazed and rested until it was time for me to go home for the evening chores. I felt tremendous satisfaction putting that big check in the bank. It made me feel responsible, and my parents seemed proud of my attitude about work and money.

The excitement and promise of my last year of high school gave way to reality as I began considering my next options. Of one thing I was certain: remaining on the farm would not be one of them.

Mom and Daddy had long ago inspired me to strive for accomplishment. When I decided to go to college, they supported me in my decision and it became an attainable goal. I first thought about Washington State where Bunny was happily doing well, majoring in home economics. Here, I ran into a wall.

Physically fit and a good athlete, I decided to major in physical education to become a teacher. I enjoyed working with people, especially kids, and it seemed a natural. Bunny was appalled!

She told me that many women in that field were gay. "You don't want anything to do with P.E.!" she said.

I was surprised and concerned by this revelation, but since she was older and more experienced, I respected her opinion. Women weren't exposed to many career choices in Ten Mile; they usually chose between homemaking, teaching, or nursing. Mom recommended the latter. "You're always so sensitive to the feelings and needs of others, Isabel. You'd be a wonderful nurse." I responded to her belief in me, and the decision was made.

Izzy showing off on Champ. The 'old barn' is in the background.

Cousin Carlie on Naomi and Izzy on Champ, 1943.

Chapter 4

It had now been five-and-a-half hours since I'd had that last beer and tranquilizer. A nurse came with my dinner on a tray, but I wasn't interested. It would be a while before I would eat. Bunny went to her motel when it got dark. I lay rigidly on my back in the detox room staring at the ceiling. The night was going to be a long one. I wasn't at all sure I could endure it.

The shivering and inner shaking got worse. They gave me small doses of librium, but I went repeatedly to the nurses' station to ask if they could give me anything more. They firmly but gently ordered me back to bed.

The nightmare was only beginning.

My body was absolutely rigid, screaming for relief. The fetal position helped. When I could no longer endure the fetal position I lay flat on my back, arms straight down at my sides, hands clenched in a fist, and jaw tense to help control the inner shaking. Sleep was impossible. I focused on holding out until morning. I would call my sons. I knew they would come get me, and take me someplace else where I could be knocked out and not have to go through this torture. I didn't know that heavy sedation was not a safe option for me at that point.

The hours dragged on relentlessly. As I stared at the window, I was relieved to see the beginning of daylight. As it grew lighter, I began to feel that I could make it a little longer. I didn't call my sons.

Bunny's support meant everything to me those first few days. She flew back to Montana on Sunday when I got a roommate and began my second phase of treatment. My roommate's name was Elsie and we shared a tiny, Spartan room. It held two narrow single beds, a tiny desk, and one straight-backed chair.

Smoking wasn't permitted, except in limited areas. This increased my discomfort and I couldn't believe that they wouldn't even let this be easy for me. A nearly military routine was an integral part of treatment. It was such a contrast to the spa-like atmosphere I had envisioned. We were required to do everything by the clock. We were awakened each morning at 5:30 and were to shower, make our beds, and be downstairs for breakfast on time. The last thing I expected from treatment was to be making my own bed and having to report to someone. Again, I was reminded that my role had changed. I was no longer making the rules. I was following them.

After breakfast we lined up for roll call and walked to the YWCA, where we attempted to play volleyball and basketball and do some calisthenics. My legs were swollen and heavy, and I was constantly out of breath. Still I tried. I was one of the slower ones, but wasn't reprimanded for not keeping up. Exercise was part of the required treatment. I was frankly shocked that they would push me physically to this extent when I felt so ill, but they kept encouraging us and didn't take no for an answer.

The regimentation reminded me of nurses training. I resented it now as I had resented it then.

▼ ▲ ▼

I applied and was accepted into the Army Cadet Nurse Corps shortly before the end of World War II. I attended classes at Providence School of Nursing in Everett, Washington, only seventy miles from home. Because the war created a need for nurses, the government paid full tuition, room and board, and books for all students in this program. It was marvelous for less fortunate women who otherwise might not have had the opportunity to go beyond high school. My financial position was stronger than most, but it was a great help to have all expenses paid. We also received a monthly fifteen-dollar stipend.

My cousin Carlie drove me to Everett in early September after tearful goodbyes. I knew as we left that Mom and Daddy and the farm would never be mine again in the same way, yet the pain I felt in pulling away was tempered by the excitement of facing the unknown. I looked forward to new friends and new experiences. Carlie dropped me off at the school entrance and I was suddenly on my own.

After registering, I received my schedule of classes and a room assignment. And I got a roommate. Her name was Bobbie Anderson. She was the tidiest person I'd ever met. Even tidier than Mom. I passed the daily room inspection performed by the nuns, but I never passed muster with Bobbie. We became great friends, more so after we had separate rooms.

Providence was a Catholic school with a somewhat more than formal atmosphere. I had usually been called Izzy by friends and classmates. Here the instructors and nuns addressed us as "Miss," and I now became "Miss Muenscher." This was soon shortened to "Minch" by classmates when staffers weren't around. First names were not used by anyone.

There were approximately thirty students in my class. Some were too cosmopolitan for me at first because of their smoking and drinking, a behavior I was philosophically opposed to at the time. Still, I developed many close friendships.

One of my best friends was Dorothy Jenny, a fellow Protestant and an excellent student. We found much in common with our love of the outdoors, horses, and shared spiritual values. She was slender, quiet, and a loner by nature. Her no-nonsense attitude did not tolerate idle chatter. She carried herself with confidence, was the blondest blond I ever saw, and had freckles everywhere. Jenny was from Stanwood, where her dad was a logger and her mother worked in a bakery. They had a lovely home and it was a treat to visit them. We had many adventures together and I treasured our closeness.

A little later, Ardelle Marchand and I also became good friends. She was bright and attractive and popular with the other girls. People were drawn to her positive attitude and enthusiasm for so many things. She was outspoken in her beliefs, a devout Catholic, and a good student. Marchand was far more sophisticated than I was, and hung out with the more cosmopolitan crowd. It took awhile for me to get to know her, but once I did, I could see what a special person she was, and valued our friendship.

The first three months of school seemed designed to test us. Classes were long, assignments difficult and demanding. Familiar faces began to disappear, and by the time we received our caps and pins, my class was down to twenty. The reasons for leaving varied, but were usually a combination of scholastic, physical, or emotional stress due to the pressure. I set my goals and did well, but the price I paid for success was an emotional one. I missed my freedom and the outdoor life on the farm. Thinking about Daddy, my horse, or Mom's abundant meals sometimes drove me to tears. I began to envy those who dropped out to return home.

I was so homesick, I caught the bus for Ten Mile whenever we had free time, even if it was only for a few hours. My dirty laundry would come with me, and Mom would wash, iron, and mail it back. I often took a classmate along. Jenny or Marchand were the most frequent visitors. Sometimes it would be Anderson, or one of the others, and I occasionally paid their fare because it would have been impossible for them to come otherwise.

My savings were still intact. Daddy would frequently corner me, give me a big hug, and press a ten dollar bill into my hand. Mom's regular letters or boxes of goodies often contained money. Their generosity and the fifteen-dollar stipend provided more than enough for me to get by. I had enough money to sometimes treat my friends to hamburgers at Mel's Diner.

While I enjoyed much of what went on at Providence, there was an uncomfortable spiritual aspect to my being there. Pastor Keller had been outspoken about his concerns when he learned of my plan to attend a Catholic school. He felt the experience would bring confusion and turmoil into my faith, possibly distancing me from God and my church. His words often came to mind during that time.

I had expected to attend an Everett Lutheran Church on Sundays, but could do so only rarely when off duty. Providence made no special arrangements for Protestants, requiring early morning chapel attendance and participation in liturgical prayers. I grew to resent this challenge to my values with some bitterness.

However, I began to adjust to my new environment as our three-month probation drew to a close. It was exciting to realize I was developing a love of nurses training, and though classes were becoming more challenging, they were interesting and stimulating. A strong support group developed with my new friends, and I felt a rising confidence that I had chosen the right career.

And then things got complicated.

Al was discharged from the Army Air Corps after the war and we resumed dating. Hank gave him his old truck-driving job and he moved in with his parents in Lynden. Distance, combined with my busy schedule, limited our opportunities to be together.

Al soon presented me with an engagement ring, at first agreeing to wait until I graduated before we would be married. However, it wasn't long before he became impatient and pressured me to marry him right away. I agreed reluctantly, knowing Providence would require me to drop out of the training program.

Sister Repparoto, the Superintendent of Nursing, found out about my plans and took me aside. She told me how well she thought I was doing, that she believed I had a special aptitude for nursing, and that it would be a shame if I dropped out. She offered me a special two-week leave to think about it before making a final decision and I agreed, leaving my things at school.

I went home and told my folks I had come back to get married. Mom and Daddy were shocked. Daddy didn't say much, but I could tell he was disappointed. Mom, however, said a great deal, alternating between angry outbursts and tears. She wanted me to have the education she hadn't been able to have. She didn't understand why Al couldn't wait until I finished school. The turmoil finally became unbearable and I moved in with Eleanor. She thought I was doing the right thing.

I went back to the potato fields, not because I needed the money, but in order to think and have something to do. Planting was hard work in the cold and rain, and I began to face reality. Married life for me in Lynden could be as a homemaker like Eleanor, or a field worker as I was now. Neither of these options seemed particularly appealing, but I gritted my teeth and planted potatoes.

The two-week leave came to an end and I rode into Providence with Hank, still intending to pick up my belongings and leave school. He dropped me off, promising to pick me up on his way back from Seattle that evening. I went to my room and collapsed on the bed in tears. After hours of anguish, torn between my commitment to Al and a career, I decided to risk losing him. I wrote him a carefully worded letter, pleading with him for understanding. I assured him of my love and asked him to wait for me to finish nursing school. I sent the letter home with Hank.

I loved Al, and our next meeting hurt me terribly. We argued, and he said he would break our engagement if I wouldn't marry him immediately. I refused and he demanded his ring. I gave it to him.

I returned to school, got up every morning, hoping I would hear from Al, hoping he would change his mind, but he didn't call and the increased work load became a blessing. I buried myself in study. As time passed, my confidence gradually returned. I found I could truly help people through my nursing and I was good at it. Things brightened considerably when Daddy arranged for me to have Champ nearby.

I had told Daddy that Dorothy Jenny boarded her horse at the fairgrounds in Everett. I assume he and Mom decided that having Champ close would help me get over Al and would ease my homesickness. They were right.

Daddy hired a trucker to bring Champ to Everett, and he paid the thirty-dollar-a-month board bill. I felt fortunate. Jenny and I rode together in our spare time and the pain began to fade. I heard little about Al until someone told me he had begun dating my cousin, Erna, soon after we broke up.

I first saw them together when Bunny and Pete were married in June of that year. I was the maid of honor, and baby sister , Elinor, who was six, was flower girl. Plans for their wedding had been made while Al and I were still engaged, and he had been asked to be an usher. He came with Erna and I felt hurt anew watching them together at the reception. I couldn't wait to leave.

My feelings were still raw and I longed for him. Aunt Essie sensed my pain and took me home with her. She held me while tears came and assured me I was beautiful, and okay, and that I would someday love again. She said I needed to get on with my life, and I knew she was right.

I devoted myself to my education. My first department experience was in obstetrics and then surgery. I began dating again in 1946, about the time I was assigned to Firland's Tuberculosis Sanitarium, which was in Seattle.

I wore one of Bunny's formals to the Providence junior/senior prom where I had my first alcohol, a pink lady. It was a spectacular evening and Marchand began giving me smoking lessons. I was becoming quite sophisticated. I had forgotten my vows never to smoke or drink.

I spent much of my free time at the fairgrounds with Champ. There, I saw and fell in love with a beautiful Tennessee Walker colt. I wrote home for my money because I had to own him. The letter from home did not contain money, but instead gave me reasons why I shouldn't buy this horse. I was persistent and the money soon arrived. I bought the colt and named him Verigo, contrived from "very gaited." This purchase almost depleted my savings account. I now spent my free time working with Verigo.

During our vacation Jenny and I took a trip into the Cascades on horseback. Verigo was too young for such a trip so I left him boarded in Everett. We started on horseback in the evening from the stables. Our destination for the next day was Stanwood, about thirty miles away, where we would meet Jenny's dad and continue the trip. We planned to ride to the North Everett waterfront park to camp the first night.

As we approached the park a man came out of a ditch and exposed himself. He terrified both Jenny and me. We rode fast and hard away from the park into the dusk of the evening. I looked over my shoulder constantly in fear, thinking he might be following us in a car. And then the traffic became heavy, spooking the horses and making them skittish. We rode a torturous ten miles, across the bridge and over the river into Marysville, where we found a corn patch that looked safe. We tied the horses to a tree and went into the center of the corn field to bed down for the night, hoping we would be hidden. In the morning I woke up with a man standing over me and I thought, "Oh my God, this is it." It turned out to be the man who owned the corn field. He was pleasant to us when we told him what had happened and why we were hiding there.

That day, we rode on to Stanwood and met up with Jenny's dad and cousin, Shirley. The horses were trucked to the foothills of the Cascades where we met Jenny's Uncle Elmer and we continued our trip into the mountains. There were four horses for the five of us, and we took turns hiking. During one of my turns to walk, Champ's hoof missed the trail. He threw Jenny's dad, Fred. I watched as Fred grabbed hold of a tree branch and freed himself of Champ as the horse hurled and crashed down the side of the mountain. Thank God, Fred was safe. Champ went tumbling uncontrollably down the steep hill. Only a few small ledges slowed his descent. He tried repeatedly to regain his footing.

By then I was screaming, afraid Champ would die. Jenny was beside herself, mistakenly thinking her dad was beneath the horse. Champ finally landed on a log and straddled it. He was hundreds of feet down the mountain and I could see his big body shaking and preparing for the next lunge. Fred said we wouldn't get Champ up the mountain again. He gently but firmly told me that he intended to shoot him and put him out of his misery. I frantically begged Fred to help me try to bring Champ up. I knew he feared for my safety but I assured him that I could talk Champ up the mountain if they would help pull. He reluctantly agreed, and handed me one end of a rope. I scrambled down to Champ and put the rope on as Fred directed. The others on top used a tree as leverage and used the tension on the rope to steady Champ as he lunged uphill.

Trying to be calm and controlled, I stayed close to him, touching his shaking body and talking to him each time he stopped. What a victory and how joyful and relieved I felt when he finally was back on the trail! Miraculously, we could find no serious injuries. The remainder of the trip, Champ was used as a pack horse.

I felt terror at times as he clambered along the trail with frying pans clapping and part of a hoof hanging over the edge as he carelessly trotted around a corner to catch up with the lead. As much as I loved him, it was hard for me to admit that Champ was not a safe horse for mountainous trails. Except for the frightening episodes, the trip was a wonderful experience. I returned to Everett refreshed and ready to resume my duties.

That summer of 1947 was eventful in another way. I met Frank. He had his own goals and yet respected mine. He was a veteran, majoring in education at the University of Washington. Although quite serious, he was a gentle, conservative type who was easy to be around. I knew Frank was a good man, and knew that we could make a good life together. He gave me a diamond ring that fall and I took him home to meet my family. I had already met his. Both our families seemed delighted with our engagement.

We were able to see more of each other when I began pediatric training in Seattle. Our relationship seemed comfortable and secure until one night in November when Al called. The sound of his voice and his invitation to go out for a Coke left my heart pounding. I was elated to be with him! We went to his hotel room and talked. Al held me in his arms and said he loved me, that he had always loved me, and I said I felt the same about him.

"Marry me, Isabel, not later, right now."

Although it was against school rules in those days for student nurses to be married, some did so secretly. Al was now willing to let me finish nurses training, providing I was willing to take the risk to marry immediately. I said yes.

I told Jenny that night and she agreed to be my attendant and help me plan the wedding. My first task was to see Frank and return his ring. I know my sudden decision both surprised and disappointed him, but no harsh words were spoken.

Al's task was no less difficult. He had to confront Erna and our two families. I know Erna loved Al just as I did. I wrote my parents and invited them to the wedding, but didn't ask their permission. Al and I asked all those involved not to tell anyone so as not to jeopardize my nurses training. We got the marriage license and agreed to meet three days later for the wedding.

I wanted a pre-marital physical. I looked forward to sex on my wedding night and to ensure a painless and pleasurable experience, I went to a doctor in Everett to have my hymen stretched, cut or broken.

I had once seen a woman come into the hospital hemorrhaging from a hymen that had been punctured on her honeymoon. Jenny and I took a bus back to Everett thirty miles north of Seattle for my exam with a highly respected doctor.

Jenny waited in the outer office while I went in. The doctor seemed to have a problem with the puncture as it took him longer than I thought it should. I sat up and was shocked to see the protrusion of his enlarged penis in front of me. He had been trying to break my hymen with his penis. I jumped off the table, shaking and quivering, grabbed my clothes and got away as fast as I could. He remained calm and tried to slow me down. I walked out, still shaking.

On our return bus ride, I told Jenny, in detail, what had happened. I couldn't control my shaking. We discussed our options and agreed I must keep the incident quiet. I had gone there for a pre-marital physical which I had no business getting while I was in nurses training. I must remain silent or my nursing days would be over. I was confident I was not the only virgin to see him for a pre-marital physical or for other reasons. I now had concern for other women as well. I was furious that a man could get away with this, but I knew I was powerless to do anything about it. I threw myself into preparing for my approaching wedding.

I had a lot to do. I made arrangements for a church, a minister, and a photographer, and reserved a motel room for the wedding night. I specifically looked for a place with a kitchenette because I wanted to start my first day of married life by fixing breakfast for Al. I asked some of my friends at school for step-by-step instructions on preparing bacon and eggs. I'd never cooked a breakfast in my life!

Jenny and I shopped for food and took it to the motel ahead of time. We also bought me a new suit, shoes, and hat, and ordered a corsage. The arrangements drained my bank account, but I was euphoric.

The three days sped by and it seemed no time at all until we all met at the church. Al, Jenny, her boyfriend Bernie, the minister, and I were all there. Daddy arrived by taxi just before the service. I later learned Mom had taken to her bed. She simply couldn't deal with it. Daddy gave me away and pressed a hundred dollar bill into my hand as he left.

"Remember, Baby, I'll always be here for you. I love you."

Izzy's parents, Fritz and Neldia Muenscher, on the front porch of the farmhouse, about 1945.

Izzy in nursing cap and cape, 1946.

Chapter 5

I was both happy and excited when Al and I went to dinner with Jenny and Bernie that evening. We had just left the church and my dreams had become reality; I looked forward to the future with great anticipation.

Al and I were sitting in the back seat of Bernie's car when I unconsciously reached for a cigarette. The tension of the day was easing and I wanted to unwind. Al grabbed the cigarette out of my hand and threw it out the window. "Hey, no smoking!" he said. I laughed, thinking he was kidding and lit up another, but his serious objection to my smoking became obvious when he disposed of this cigarette in the same way. I was shocked! We hadn't talked about this. I had assumed he didn't mind.

I seldom lit a cigarette after that without his physically taking it away. This experience on our wedding day began an uneasiness which would later add to my regret at marrying.

Even our wedding night turned into a disaster. I thought lovemaking was going to be wonderful, but it hurt and I was scared. The pain, plus the worry I felt at keeping our marriage a secret provoked tears I couldn't control.

I tried to fix a nice breakfast the next morning, but nothing I did came out right. The bacon was limp, too raw, and greasy; the egg yolks broke and were cooked too hard; everything was soaked in bacon fat. Al didn't say anything. It was simply unsatisfactory and I knew it. Our marriage, thus far, had consisted of unsuccessful lovemaking and bad food. And for me, no smoking.

I was relieved when our first forty-eight hours together ended. Al returned to Lynden and I went back to my hospital residence. The rest of the week was uneventful. Then I received a message from Sister Marie at Providence. I was to report to Everett immediately.

Sister Marie had replaced Sister Repparato as my supervisor, and I found her standing with her back to me as I walked into her office. "Miss Muenscher," she said, coldly, "I understand you are married." She handed me a note addressed to Isabel Muenscher Jansen from a member of the Ten Mile community, congratulating me on my marriage.

"Yes, I am, sister," I replied, resignedly, shocked that she had learned of my marriage.

"You have broken the rules and must leave." The finality in her voice was frightening.

"Please let me stay," I pleaded, "I'll do anything if you'll let me finish."

"No," she said adamantly, "You must pack immediately and go."

"Can I transfer my credits to another school?"

"No, you may not. Your credits will never leave Providence."

I couldn't believe it was happening. A number of girls in my nursing program had managed to keep their marriages secret. Why had this happened to me? I couldn't discuss this with Sister Marie, but it seemed so harsh.

I was devastated and felt a great sense of loss as I packed my belongings. My career in nursing had come to mean so much. Now it was over and I had yet another reason to regret my decision to marry. There was nothing to do but call Al. I don't remember how I got to Lynden.

My life now became so complicated and filled with conflicting thoughts that I made no attempt to search for another nursing school. I was so afraid that Sister Marie had destroyed my records. I didn't want to find out that it might be true.

I moved into the Jansen's big family home with Al. It was a busy place. Al was the eighth of twelve children and many of them were still living at home. His mother was called "Moeder," and his father went by the initials "G.J." They had both been raised in Holland. G.J. spoke fairly good English, but Moeder wasn't as easy to understand.

Moeder worked very hard. I asked her what I could do to help and she put me to work ironing baskets of white shirts. All the brothers in the family wore these starched white shirts regularly. I stood for hours ironing them and then re-ironing my failures. Their household routine was tedious and unfamiliar, and I felt humiliated by my slow progress in learning my tasks.

Moeder was away one day when G.J. came in with a whole chicken for me to prepare. He watched me struggle with it for a few minutes and then offered to help. I was grateful, but felt inadequate, knowing he had expected more from me. I didn't know it was one of those chickens which required roasting for long periods in an oven. We cut it up, breaded it in flour, and I fried it the way I had seen Mom do it. It looked pretty good in the frying pan.

The usual complement of six or eight family members gathered for the meal. I soon noticed they were having difficulty chewing. All the pieces of fried chicken were tough and raw in the center. Nothing was said, but they didn't eat it. I had been embarrassed by my poor ironing ability, but this new failure was even more humiliating. It seemed I couldn't do the simplest things in this new and strange environment. I wondered what Moeder was telling her competent daughters about me, but they always treated me well, so perhaps I shouldn't have worried.

Al worked long hours, still driving truck for Hank. He left around three each morning and returned at three or four in the afternoon. It was difficult for the two of us to have any privacy, with so many people living together.

Eleanor and Hank sensed this and invited us to make an apartment out of their basement recreation room. They lived only a few blocks from the Jansen home. It was cramped, but we welcomed the privacy. The basement consisted of one room with a small sink built into a bar on one side, but no cooking or bathroom facilities. I cooked on a little hot plate and occasionally used Eleanor's oven.

It was helpful to be close to her. She taught me basic homemaking and how to make simple meals. Al never seemed to get tired of the macaroni and cheese casseroles I alternated with spaghetti for our dinners. I made tuna sandwiches for his lunch nearly every day.

I settled into the domestic routine as best I could, but I was unhappy and longed to be back at school. Al's early departure each morning allowed me to sleep in. I would get up late to face dishes and chores put off from the previous day. Mornings became depressing and unfulfilling. I would work for a while and then go upstairs to help Eleanor with their two children, Heidi and Jimmy.

A few weeks before Al and I had married, Bill, Al's twin brother, had married Be Covalt. Be was one of the first visitors to our little apartment. I liked her immediately. She was bouncy and creative and used colorful language. We had even more in common when we discovered our mothers had gone to school together in Bellingham. Be's father had been District Attorney at Whatcom County some time in the 1940s. Be became a close friend, and I admired her ability to speak up for herself. She smoked when she wanted to—in front of anyone, including Al, and didn't let Bill push her around.

The Jansens weren't heavy drinkers, but they served alcohol regularly in their homes. Al and I didn't keep nor serve alcohol in our apartment at first, but I began to look forward to going out or visiting the Jansens when I knew alcohol would be served. My first alcoholic drink had been the pink lady at Providence's Junior/Senior Prom before I was married. I had associated that alcohol with glamour and sophistication. I had none of these associations when I drank alcohol with the Jansens, but it relieved my feelings of uselessness for an evening. I loved the way it made me feel.

Six weeks after we were married, Al and I spent Christmas with my parents and brought a fifth of bourbon with us as a gift. I didn't immediately realize what a turn-about this was for me. I had not only brought alcohol into my parents home, but encouraged Daddy to drink it, a behavior which would have horrified me a few months earlier.

This disturbed Mom and began building a wall between us. I started shifting the fear and guilt I felt at drinking alcohol to her, believing she was the cause of Daddy's drinking problem by not serving alcohol in their home.

My sudden and obvious change in attitude toward alcohol must have alarmed and confused members of my family, but no one said anything to me.

I'm sure that my family was concerned about more than my drinking. Al's sense of humor, which had originally attracted me, soon turned against me. I became the target of his sarcasm and the butt of his jokes when other people were present. His behavior around other people embarrassed me, but when I tried to discuss this with him in private, he responded in anger. Eventually, his standard response during any disagreement was to suggest that I pack my bags and leave. As a result, I stopped telling him my feelings and was cautious about confronting him on anything he might interpret as criticism.

My sister Bunny and I were living in close proximity since my marriage to Al. I sensed her concern about me, but I didn't want her to know how unhappy I was. She never said anything. Still there was a new awkwardness between us.

December of that year, Bunny and Pete's baby girl, Jane Ann, was born. She was a beautiful baby and my first niece. I often babysat for her, and Bunny would call me if Jane was sick. Baby Jane became a bright spot in my life at a time when I needed one. I loved the way she responded to me, and we still have a special closeness.

Because of the new tensions I felt when I was with my family, I discovered that I was more comfortable around the Jansens. They didn't care that I had quit nursing school, nor did they think anything of me having a drink. A tight-knit family, they not only spent their free time together, they were supportive of one another in business, too.

The Jansen family was in the landscaping and retail flower business. Of the twelve children, about half of them ended up being involved in this kind of work. Be's husband, Bill, worked for his brother, Gary, at "Jansen's Flowers" in Bellingham. He was creative, had loads of artistic talent, and did very well. G.J. sold the original Jansen Landscaping Flower Shop to Al's oldest brother, Jack, and also sold him some land at nearby Wiser Lake.

Soon after Al and I were married, Jack moved the business to Wiser Lake and G.J. began construction on a new home there. Al decided that we, too, should build a house at Wiser Lake. He bought an acre of land from his father, but I couldn't get excited about the prospect of a new house. I couldn't help financially because Al didn't want me to work, and that dependency, too, bothered me.

Al was probably not aware of how I felt about this proposed move. He never asked and I didn't tell him. I wasn't ready for the responsibility of a new house, and I knew that at Wiser Lake I would become even more isolated. I would no longer be able to drop by

Eleanor's, nor walk to the store. Instead I would become more dependent on Moeder and G.J. for companionship. And to get to the grocery store, I would have to ask G.J. or Al's brother, Everett, for a ride.

In addition to what little independence I had, I was also about to lose Champ and Verigo. They were still in Everett where I owed back boarding charges. Al was angry at this added expense. Daddy's refusal to help surprised me. He told me I was now a married woman and should look to Al for support. My argument that Al had no interest in my horses fell on deaf ears and I felt shocked and hurt at this new reality. Al reluctantly paid to have them brought to Lynden where I found an inexpensive field to rent, but it didn't work out. The fences were poor and I was continually being called to get them out of the road or someone's yard.

The worry and conflict finally became too much and I turned the horses over to Carlie, who took care of selling them. I spent many tearful days thinking about Champ and Verigo and all the other things I had given up for marriage. I longed to be back in nurses training where I had felt satisfied with my life.

Chapter 6

It was becoming clear to me that my fantasies of Al over the past several years had not been based on reality. We were unable to maintain any real intimacy. My feelings and goals were unimportant to Al and I felt continually belittled. I grieved the loss of my freedom, my nursing career and the closeness I had felt with Mom and Daddy. I also grieved for the marriage I had fantasized having—the wholesome, trusting, loving kind that I would now never have.

My days seemed pointless. I knew that I needed to contribute something, and all there seemed to be was cooking and cleaning. Even though there wasn't much of this, it was drudgery.

I began dreading Mom and Daddy's visits. I knew they could see how unfulfilled and unhappy I was. Their hopes for me had been shattered, and I hated seeing the hurt and concern in their eyes. They must have sensed some of this because they always called to warn me of their coming. It took all my energy to clean up the apartment we were now renting and pretend everything was okay in their presence.

My addiction to cigarettes was a temporary escape. I knew I was dependent on them. I no longer attempted to light one when Al was around, but smoked whenever I could.

Uncomfortable with my role as I was, I still felt strongly about my commitment to Al. I contemplated divorce, but my upbringing and family values made it an unthinkable option. When Al began talking about a baby, I liked the idea. I discontinued birth control that spring and by June was pregnant with Patti. Smoking was impossible for me during my pregnancy, since cigarettes made me violently ill. The detrimental effects of smoking on unborn babies were not known then, and I missed the comfort smoking provided me.

Al and some family members began designing our Wiser Lake house. I had no talent for planning a house and couldn't seem to get interested enough to even let my own preferences be known. We moved out of the apartment when construction began and lived in the unfinished attic in G.J.'s new home in Wiser Lake to save money.

Skip, Al's youngest brother, and his wife, Lou, lived in the basement. Lou was pregnant with their second child. I helped her care for baby Steve and with other household chores. My nurse's training in postnatal and infant care was finally put to use. This suspended my nagging feelings of uselessness.

My bout with morning sickness was beginning to subside when we moved again. This time it was to Bellingham to take care of Al's sister, Marie, and her new baby, Marsha. Again, I felt needed, and I enjoyed being with Marie and her husband.

Then Jack, Al's oldest brother, and his wife, Peggy, had their fifth child, Jill. We moved in with them so I could help out. They had a two-bedroom apartment behind the flower shop at Wiser Lake and we shared a bedroom with their kids. It was crowded, but at least I felt useful.

I was still pregnant when we moved into our new house. There was little joy for me in the move. I began to feel unimportant again and I couldn't shake the feeling that I was trapped in my marriage.

When I was three weeks past due, I finally went to the hospital in Bellingham to have labor induced. My beautiful daughter Patti was born that afternoon about four o'clock. I looked at her as she was placed in my arms and was not prepared for the weight of responsibility that flooded over me. I felt a moment of fear as the tears rolled down my cheeks, but the weight lifted as suddenly as it had come and was replaced by elation and an overwhelming sense of love and protectiveness.

Patti blended so completely into my life that taking care of her was never a problem. She was my treasure and I enjoyed her company from the very beginning.

Soon after Patti was born, Bill, Al's twin, and Be decided to open their own flower shop in Longview, Washington. Be's dad, Harley Covalt, and "Mamita," her stepmother, agreed to help finance it. Their new business prospered immediately with Bill's experience and Be's creative artistry.

Al had often spoken of his dissatisfaction with truck driving and I began to encourage him to start a business as Bill and Be had done. We visited them, saw how well they were doing, and decided to move to Longview to start a landscaping service. Al sold our Wiser Lake house to his brother, Jack, and we used the profit to open the business in Longview. It was 1950 and Patti was one year old. Bill and Be had an explosive relationship, but Be was fun to be around and we spent a lot of time together.

Al worked hard and managed to get several small landscaping contracts that summer while I ran a sales yard in downtown Longview. We sold shrubs and bedding plants to do-it-yourselfers. Our lot also provided plants for Al's jobs and I drove our pickup on weekly trips to Portland to replace stock. It was stimulating to be away from Bellingham and to be involved in a business. My regrets began to fade. Al seemed satisfied with our relationship, and our main source of friction was the fact that I had resumed smoking after Patti's birth.

Naïvely, that fall we moved our operation to Beaverton, Oregon, in search of a bigger market. Al got several small gardening jobs, enough to make expenses, but no one knew him or his work and we weren't successful. The bigger market was there, but we had no sales yard and no name recognition, and in such a large place, without time and money, there was no way for us to develop a business.

Patti and I had a great time that summer, however, and it was probably the happiest period in our marriage for Al and me. With no family or friends nearby, we began relying on each other for companionship.

I kept the apartment clean and prepared evening meals while Al was working. Patti and I spent the rest of the time playing outside in the sun. I felt more content that summer than I had since our wedding, and when Al said he wanted another child I stopped using contraceptives. I was pregnant with Freddy by September.

We gave up on the Beaverton business and moved back to Longview late that fall where Al tried to resume his landscaping business, without much success. We lived on our meager accounts receivable as long as we could. I was terrified when the money ran out and Al didn't get a job to see us through, but we didn't go hungry. Bill and Be were still doing quite well and I was grateful to get the bags of groceries they brought us.

My friend from Providence, Dorothy Jenny, had married Bernie Knutzen by this time and they came to Longview to visit us. They were on their way to work for his father on a potato farm in eastern Washington. Bernie told us about a large military housing complex being built at Moses Lake. He thought Al might have an opportunity to get a landscaping contract there with the government. Al looked into it and formed a partnership with his brother Jack to make the bid. Jack had the necessary funds and bonding ability for such a large undertaking. They got the job.

Our baby was due in June of 1951. The contract was granted in early spring. It was a financial breakthrough for us and we moved to Moses Lake in March. Having Jenny and Bernie nearby was a comfort. Their baby, Jeff, was a year old and my Patti was two. Both Jenny and I were pregnant, and our friendship grew even stronger.

Al's bid of sixty thousand dollars for the job seemed an astronomical sum of money to me, and I guess it was, in those days. It changed our standard of living dramatically. We rented a nice two-bedroom apartment that was light and airy, but our privacy disappeared when Al hired several friends and acquaintances from Lynden and Whatcom County to work on the job.

I suddenly found myself running a boarding house.

The project was going well, but our marriage wasn't. Everything happened too fast. There was a constant flow of people through the house. There were endless parties every weekend which sometimes spilled over into the middle of the week. Hard liquor and beer were constants.

On May 17th, five weeks early, Dean Frederick was born. He weighed six pounds and was strong and very active. I took him home a day later. My new baby was not content. Nor was I. He often suffered from upset stomach, spit up frequently, had diarrhea, and was a constant concern. In contrast, Patti continued to be healthy, happy and relaxed.

Three weeks after Freddy's birth, Bunny called to say that my Uncle Carl had died suddenly. He had seemed to be in good health and strong, and was working with Daddy on the old barn when he died. Bunny said they suspected a heart attack. Uncle Carl was only fifty-six-years-old. Al and I took Patti and the new baby to Ten Mile for the funeral.

Bunny called again a few weeks later to tell me Uncle Walter had suffered a serious stroke in New York. He was fifty-nine and would no longer be able to continue his work at Cornell University, where he had taught for thirty years.

Again she called. Daddy had fallen off a scaffold and broken his leg. He had been trying to finish the work he and Uncle Carl had started on the barn. She said he would heal all right, but would have to wear a leg cast.

I was beginning to dread Bunny's phone calls.

I worried about Daddy's overall health. In a matter of weeks one brother had died and the other was incapacitated. Could Daddy be next?

Aside from the fact that Uncle Carl had been Daddy's best friend and Daddy would miss him so much, I knew that he would worry over the two farms that would now be run by Uncle Carl's sons, Carlie and Bobby. I worried about how the added stress would affect him. Because of my changed attitude toward alcohol, it didn't even occur to me to worry about Daddy drinking again. Fortunately, he didn't.

Al and I continued to have three or four men living with us in our two-bedroom apartment. I hired a woman to help me cook and take care of the children. We seemed to be doing laundry constantly. She came in the morning and left just before dinner.

Many evenings were spent drinking and dancing. Now that I was no longer pregnant, I joined in wholeheartedly as soon as Patti and Freddy were in bed. I often drank sufficient amounts to make me sick or give me a hangover. I knew it wasn't right, that it wasn't acceptable behavior, but it just seemed to happen.

Jenny and I remained close friends, and I saw her almost daily. She went into labor on November fifth and I drove her to the hospital. As usual at this tiny hospital, there was only one nurse on duty. Jenny's doctor, who had delivered Freddy a few months earlier, knew that I was a nurse. We had arranged ahead of time that I would assist at Jenny's delivery. When she began to hemorrhage I thought, "Oh

God, please don't let her die." She was given a blood transfusion and both she and her son did fine.

The landscape project was completed in late fall, providing Jack and Al with a nice profit. I had adjusted to living in eastern Washington and didn't want to leave Jenny, but completing the job meant moving on to something else.

Al invested most of our share of the Moses Lake profits in a sawmill in Newport, Oregon, where we bought a small house. The mill was a three-way partnership and a larger business than anything we had done before. It required a CPA to handle the books. Al no longer needed my help with records or with managing a boarding house. I was back to keeping house and taking care of the children. I was soon lonely again.

Be visited us shortly after we moved to Newport and shocked me with the news that she planned to divorce Al's brother, Bill. She had her reasons. We had long known of their personality conflicts, but Be's stepmother and father had invested money in their business to get them started, and I assumed she would be stuck; but not so.

Be moved to Seattle after the divorce and went to work for a department store. I was a product of traditional values and I marveled at these unexpected events. I had talked little to anyone about how trapped and angry I felt about my life, but Be's independence made me think.

I was doing what I knew others expected of me. I was keeping my marriage together as I had been conditioned to do. But I had also been keeping my needs to myself and had demanded little of Al.

Al had made it quite clear that he didn't want me to work. I was to take care of the children and house, and to be there when he needed me. Our financial position was secure. Still, my need to work and contribute to something greater than self and a traditional home left me with an unsurmountable frustration.

I began looking through newspapers for nursing opportunities. I lacked confidence and worried that I had been away from nurses training too long, but I saw an ad placed by a new doctor who had recently moved to Newport, and I went to see him. He listened as I told him about my background and he hired me when I told him I wanted to work limited hours at minimum pay for the experience.

Al wasn't as difficult to deal with as I had anticipated when I told him about my new schedule. I would be working five days a week from nine to two, and would have sufficient time to take care of my obligations at home before and after work.

On a day-to-day basis, my job didn't affect Al too much. When he wanted me to be free to travel with him, however, there was trouble. He was angry and frustrated that I put my job ahead of him and didn't want to go.

In the midst of this, Al found that the sawmill no longer needed his attention. He bid a large landscaping project in Richland,

Washington and was awarded the job. It meant we would have to move again. I resisted. I didn't want to leave Newport. I had thought we would live there forever. I had resented our previous migratory existence and hated to again move to a place where I would know no one.

Although marriage counseling was a new concept in 1952, I persuaded Al to attend a session in Portland with me. He was reluctant, but finally agreed. Al spent the entire session focusing on what was wrong with me, not the marriage. Despite the fact that the therapist told us that he could see little hope for our marriage without further counseling, Al flatly refused to have any part of it. I decided I would try to stick it out and made plans for the move to Richland with Al. Even as I prepared to leave my job and friends, I was consumed by despair.

The routine at Richland was dull and lonely. There were men living in our home again. I had no help, no friends, and two children to care for. Because we knew no one in Richland, I didn't even have the evening parties to look forward to. In my current state of mind, I didn't care.

I missed my nursing job. Baby Freddy must have sensed my despair. He clung to me more than ever. I spent my days with him on my hip while I did the laundry and other household chores. I continued to hide my emotions, and put up a front, pretending I was okay. When I did approach Al with my feelings, I got the same old response about packing my bags. Later, he would say to Patti, "Mommy's unhappy living with us. How would you like a new Mommy?"

I confided my feelings to my friend Jenny, who still lived in Moses Lake. I occasionally drove the one hundred miles to see her so that we might talk. She was a wonderful listener and I eventually realized that my life was not going to get better as long as I was with Al. I envisioned that my children would grow up to think it was okay to treat people with no respect, as Al treated me. And I didn't like who I was in that environment. Life seemed unbearable. I couldn't stand it any longer. I had to leave.

Finally, when the kids were with Mom and Daddy for a few days, I told Al I was leaving him. He appeared shocked and hurt, but insisted on beginning the proceedings immediately. That day, in July of 1952, I packed a few things and left.

I needed a job and a lawyer, the latter as soon as possible. Be's dad, Harley Covalt in Portland, was no longer a practicing attorney, but I called him for advice. Not only did he recommend an attorney, but he and Bessie also invited the kids and me to live with them while I looked for a job and an apartment. I accepted, grateful for their friendship. They met me at the bus station and took me home with them.

My next step was to tell Mom and Daddy. I went back to Ten

Mile. I dreaded this, for I knew their beliefs and family standards left little tolerance for divorce. I was in for a surprise.

"Thank God," Daddy said. "I wondered how long it would take you to do something about yourself." His next remark shocked me even more. "Don't ever go back to him. You've made the right decision."

They loaned me enough to tide us over until I got a job, and offered to have the kids stay longer. I knew I could have moved home with them and was tempted, but I also knew I might never be able to leave, that it might weaken my resolve to make it on my own.

The next week, Aunt Essie brought Patti and Freddy to Portland by train, and stayed a few days to take care of them at the Covalts while I looked for a job and got settled.

Al let me have the household furnishings in Richland, and while Aunt Essie stayed with the children, Bunny drove me there and helped with the packing and moving. I had dinner with Al one last time to discuss details, and when it was over I felt sick. I was really on my own.

As I had expected, Al wasn't supportive. He kept the car and bank account, leaving me with no money. He promised two hundred dollars a month to support the children, but after I received one check, the support money stopped until the divorce was final.

Not only was my marriage lost, but my cousins became distant. I had broached the topic of divorce with Cousin Eleanor before I talked to Al and had found predictable resistance. She thought it would be wrong, no matter what the cause. Eleanor had been my closest confidant during the marriage, but she said she would have nothing further to do with me if I divorced Al.

This was confirmed one weekend when I arrived to pick up Patti and Freddy at Hank and Eleanor's. She didn't even acknowledge me when I came into the house. The divorce was still pending and Al and my cousin Erna were there together. They, too, ignored me. The kids were playing some place and I wandered about, trying to find their things. Hank finally came to my rescue, helping me gather everything together and get out the door.

I had trouble eating and sleeping, and was anxious all the time. Before I knew it, my weight dropped from one-hundred-ten pounds to ninety-five.

Izzy with son Freddy and daughter Patti, 1954.

Chapter 7

The Covalts seemed to enjoy having us. I did the laundry and most of the cooking and cleaning for them in return for our board and room. The skills learned in nearly six years of marriage now became an asset.

Be's younger brother, Jim, was living at home when I moved in with the Covalts. He was three years younger than I. I had been around him from time to time, with Be, but I hadn't known him very well. Jim was a sophomore at Portland State College, majoring in sociology and attending school on the G.I. Bill. He took care of Patti and Freddy for me occasionally while I was job hunting or out looking for an apartment. We also spent a lot of time talking.

Jim had suffered a childhood illness, nephritis, and had been told not to expect to live to be much older than thirty. We shared our aspirations and fears and gradually, over the three weeks I stayed with his parents, we got to know each other.

I was relieved when a young Portland surgeon hired me as his receptionist, bookkeeper, and nurse. I was also his x-ray and lab technician. This broad scope of activity was challenging and interesting to me. I was not only relieved to get this job, but excited at the prospect of again doing something that felt worthwhile.

Through a newspaper ad, I found a couple who offered board and an unfinished attic room as well as child care while I worked. This arrangement cost two hundred dollars a month, fifty dollars less than I earned.

Alcohol became revolting to me again as I observed its effect on my new landlords. They were frequently drinking and fighting, and I was often called upon to take care of their three kids as well as my own when they went out at night.

They kept the house clean and neat and the meals were good, when there were any, but as alcohol was their priority, there was sometimes little food at all. There were days when I had to put water on cold cereal for Patti and Fred's breakfast. Because there was seldom fruit in the house, I tried to reserve enough money to occasionally treat Patti and Fred to some, but couldn't limit the small supply to my own children when the other children needed it just as much. I couldn't believe that I wasn't able to afford to even feed my kids a consistent, well-balanced diet.

It was not surprising that I couldn't sleep.

In addition to my precarious financial situation, I felt possessive of Patti and Freddy and worried constantly about Al's visitation rights. I feared he might try to take them away from me. His immediate relationship and resulting marriage to my cousin Erna added to my resentfulness and jealousy. This influenced my behavior and made things harder for all of us. I wished Al would disappear completely, but I was sure he wouldn't. He hung on to his visitation rights.

I worried, wondering if I had done the right thing in leaving Al. Was my life any better now than it was before?

The divorce was settled in August and I received the house in Newport, which we still owned, and the mortgage of forty-five hundred dollars.

The house payments were seventy-five dollars a month and I had difficulty keeping it rented. Maintenance was high and when I did get renters, they seldom paid more than sixty or sixty-five dollars a month. The cash flow was always negative, and took a big chunk out of my fifty dollars discretionary fund.

Al's child support payment, according to the court order, was to be one-hundred-fifty dollars per month, but he paid sporadically, usually late, and sometimes not until the end of the year.

Jim was my only friend in Portland, and he began dropping by to see us in the evenings. I still didn't have a car, and neither did Jim, so he occasionally borrowed his parent's car and we'd all go to a movie together or, on the weekends, we'd go for a drive.

Life became easier a few months later when I managed to put a down payment on a 1947 Plymouth, but our living conditions were unacceptable, and I placed a classified ad for a home to share.

Helen O'Connor answered the ad. She had a nice house she needed help with and two children about the same ages as Patti and Freddy. Helen and I became good friends and shared the task of taking care of the children when one of us needed to do something alone. Things began to fall into place when we hired a woman to take care of the children while we worked.

Jim continued to visit. Sometimes he would call ahead and sometimes he wouldn't, but after he managed to buy a car, he came often during the week. He was there one memorable evening when I went to the door to greet a fellow I had met through the office. We had a movie date and I came back to tell Jim I was leaving.

"Where are you going?"

I told him.

"I don't want you to do that."

"What do you mean, Jim?"

"I love you. I would rather you wouldn't date other guys."

I didn't go to the movie.

As we sat and talked that night, Jim was more assertive than I had ever seen him. The strength of his feelings surprised me. We had been good friends, but as he told me how much he cared for me and of his love, I experienced a warm emotional change within me, and it felt good. I reminded him that I was three years older, divorced, had two kids, and that he had never married. Jim was convinced this was not a problem and I began to believe him.

There were other considerations, primarily Jim's health. He was a veteran discharged after the Korean War with a forty-percent disability. The military physician had again told Jim that his life expectancy was limited, as the nephritis was expected to become active again as he got older. Sooner or later, his kidneys would stop functioning.

Dr. Wayson, my employer, put Jim through a complete physical, and though he was more optimistic about how long Jim would have, he did confirm that his kidneys would probably fail eventually. Dr. Wayson also said Jim's blood pressure was up slightly. Jim was a big man, "Big Jim Covalt," and he loved to eat. He was six-and-a-half-feet tall and weighed about two-hundred-seventy pounds. He wasn't fat, but he surely wasn't thin, either. The doctor encouraged him to diet and he lost fifty pounds, appearing quite slender.

I worried about Jim's health, but there was something about his inner strength and calm attitude that reassured me. He had a positive attitude and I found myself believing that he would live.

Even though his family liked me, Jim didn't find it that easy to convince them that our marriage was a good idea. Jim's dad and stepmother, Mamita, felt Jim should marry someone closer to his age and experience. They now became critical of me, and Mamita said our marriage would kill Jim's father. Harley became bedridden as a result of the stress over our pending wedding. I went to see him, but it did no good. He asked me to walk away from the marriage. It was a painful time for them, but Jim insisted they accept it and they finally did.

Jim's older sister, Margo Dahl, gave him a diamond that had been his mother's and he designed an engagement ring around it, presenting it to me at Christmas that year.

We were married March 5, 1954, in a Methodist church in Seattle. Mom had checked with the Lutheran pastor in Bellingham and found that he would not perform the ceremony because of my divorce. But Margo stepped in and arranged things for us in Seattle and we were able to have a traditional wedding. We were delighted, too, when Harley and Mamita attended. The reception was held at the farm in Ten Mile with a few close friends.

The addition of Jim to my family in Ten Mile was smooth from the beginning, each recognizing the trusting and caring nature of the other. Mom shared fond memories of Jim's mother with us. They had been the best of friends at Bellingham Elementary School. Because Jim had been only thirteen at the time of his mother's death, these stories meant a lot to him.

Before Jim and I were married, we had discussed how we would run our home and what our relationship would be. He understood my need to work and pursue a career and that I could not be a traditional wife and homemaker. I don't believe Jim even wanted a traditional wife; so we agreed to share responsibilities and to hire professional help as necessary to ensure a clean and happy household. These things were never an issue for us.

We agreed right then that we would be united in all decisions including those concerning the children. Jim wanted to treat Patti and Fred as his own, to be free to love and discipline them as a natural father. He wanted us to have children together, and very much wanted to adopt Patti and Freddy as well. I hoped for more children, too.

Our first home in Portland was a converted garage and we had fun fixing, cleaning, and painting it until it was comfortable. My early sewing training that had been forced on me in 4-H and high school was finally put to use making curtains. It was a tiny place, but the rent was only fifty-five dollars a month and there was a large yard with a protective hedge sheltering it from the street. The bathroom was incredibly small. We bathed the kids in a galvanized wash tub on the floor of the shower.

Jim took the kids to and from school, did the grocery shopping, and usually had our evening dinner started when I got home from work. It was a happy time for all of us and a stable, comfortable, mostly stress-free time for me. I treasured the evenings when the kids were in bed and Jim and I would sit up playing Scrabble or cribbage and sharing our thoughts and feelings.

It seemed that I discovered something new and wonderful about him each day. He had an incredible mind, and it was exciting to be around him. I knew I could depend on his gentleness and strength and I had never felt so loved. Our first year of marriage was a year of discovery for us, and it seemed we couldn't get enough of each other.

Jim was not a good money manager and was happy when I took over our finances. His G.I. Bill checks increased slightly when we were married and we improved our situation further when we sold my car. This gave us needed financial stability. Although it required careful managing, we could now make frequent trips to visit the family and the farm. Jim looked forward to the trips to Ten Mile as much as the kids and I did. We could always count on being greeted with love and open arms. We often brought fresh food back from the farm with us.

Dad Covalt never again discussed his earlier disapproval of our marriage and always treated me with respect, as did Mamita. He came often to visit us, usually in the evening by himself, and frequently joined us for a game of Scrabble. Sometimes he came loaded with gifts of canned food. This was especially welcome, considering our limited budget. We allotted forty dollars a month for groceries. Jim's daily budget for school was ten cents for coffee. He carried food with him from home.

It was my responsibility to manage and plan the meals. We ate a lot of hamburger and beans. My powdered milk mixtures gained a reputation for being lumpy. One month I miscalculated. All we had left at the end of the month were a few dried red kidney beans in the cupboard. It was scary, but Jim disappeared for a while, and then returned with a big box of food. He had arranged credit at our little local grocery store.

We all looked forward to going to Harley and Mamita's for dinner. They were now Grandpa and Grandmother Covalt. A banana from Grandmother Covalt's fruit bowl was always a treat. Jim and I would do most of the food preparation when we visited and there was often a ham, a rare delicacy for all of us.

We liked to picnic in the park or our front yard where the kids could play. Our most extravagant outings usually consisted of a drive-in movie with home-popped popcorn and Kool-Aid. One such evening Patti and Freddy were bickering in the back seat as we drove to the movie. Jim warned them to stop or we would go back home. The bickering continued and Jim surprised all of us by doing what he said he would. It was a lesson well-learned and the kids knew what to expect after that. He was always consistent and followed through, and they respected him. He was a positive influence in their lives in many ways.

Our first Christmas together was memorable. Jim told us he had work to do and suggested we sit together in the tiny bedroom and sing Christmas carols to attract Santa Claus. We sang until we heard sleigh bells and the patter of reindeer. Then Santa came in with a "Ho, ho, ho," and questions for Freddy and Patti. Had they been good? Had they been helping their mother?

The sparkling eyes of my two kids and the anticipation on their faces was exciting and exhilarating to see. Then Santa wished us a merry Christmas with a loud happy voice, said good-bye, and we heard the bells and reindeer fade into the distance. This was the first of many Christmas eves that Santa came. Unfortunately, Jim always had some task or errand that called him away at the last minute, and he never got to see Santa.

The family grew over the years and the rooms where we waited for Santa changed and became more comfortable, but it was always an important and eagerly anticipated event in our lives.

Chapter 8

Jim and I wanted to have our first child as close in age to my first two as possible, and I was pregnant three months after we married. I had tremendous fears for this unborn baby all through the pregnancy, fears I didn't share even with Jim. Some of my worries about the baby's health were well-founded. They were intensified by a health issue for the baby, because the pregnancy was complicated by RH blood factors. Jimmy was born James Harley Covalt on March 18, 1955.

He needed a complete blood change shortly after his birth. He tolerated it well and I was relieved and happy when I brought him home. The entire family, particularly Jim's parents, were attentive and excited.

Mom stayed with us a few days to help. The little house on Liberty Street was crowded and she had to sleep on the davenport near Jimmy's basket.

I had stopped working shortly before Jimmy's birth and now experienced one of the most relaxed and pleasant periods of my adult life. My relationships with Jim and the children were so meaningful. I no longer felt the fear or unworthiness I had experienced previously.

Jim got a part-time job with a detective agency to get us by until I could work again. With the slightly increased G.I. Bill check and small disability payment each month from the Veteran's Administration, we managed. Then Jim found a better paying job in the fabric section of a Portland department store and was able to bring home remnants at little or no cost. This put my sewing skills to good use and I felt well dressed and fashionable in what I made.

With Jim's encouragement, I finally transferred my credits from Providence to Portland State College. It was a wonderful surprise to get the notice that Providence still had my records and that Sister Marie's threats to obstruct their transfer had not been carried out. I started attending classes.

We did have one problem, however. One month, we were a few days late on our payment on the Newport house, and the people who held the contract started foreclosure. I was terrified. Mom and Daddy loaned us the money to pay off the house and we sold it for sixty-three-hundred dollars, netting enough to pay them back and provide a down payment on a house in Portland. It was a relief to be rid of the monthly losses and those long trips to the coast to do maintenance.

We found an older home just two blocks from our little "garage." It had a large yard, willow trees, a spot for a garden, and most importantly, more room. We moved in the fall of 1956. Jimmy was nearly two by this time and the increased space was welcome even if the slightly higher cost of living was not. Having moved only a few blocks, we didn't have to give up our old neighborhood and friends. We added new ones instead.

Jim and I both wanted more children, but the doctor had warned us after Jimmy's birth that we should not attempt another pregnancy. We looked into adoption. We were turned down because of my divorce. Since there wouldn't be another baby, I decided to go back to work. I needed something, if only part time, and I started with a rapidly expanding toy company, Baum Plastics, that sold through a party plan, much like Tupperware.

The parties and demonstrations were held in the evening when Jim could be with the kids, and I did the organizing, phoning, and bookkeeping during the day. It soon became more than a part-time effort. I sponsored others who conducted parties for me and was soon a regional supervisor, attending management, sales, and strategy meetings. My organization did so well we sometimes had more parties booked than we could attend and Jim would be drafted to go out and make a showing for me.

Soon, the company offered me the entire Seattle area to open and manage. The Portland branch had proved it could be successful, and the company had been eyeing the Seattle market for some time. I knew the Portland area manager and how substantial her income was.

Jim was still planning to get his degree, now in education, and teach. We knew he could transfer his certification to Seattle, but he was concerned that he might someday be working "for me" instead of "with me."

There was another factor that I considered privately. Jim was not Patti and Freddy's natural father. That he loved and cherished them wasn't a question, but I worried how this relationship might change over time. Plus, Jim was continually urging me to risk having another baby. I felt a responsibility to have another of Jim's children, if I could, and I didn't want having such a demanding job to interfere with that.

We decided to stay in Portland. I continued with the party business. Then an opportunity came along for Jim that would soon change our lives. The department store closed, laying him off, and he was looking for another job. He was carrying a full load at school when he was offered a part-time job as a bartender. Jim had second thoughts about working around alcohol and wasn't sure he liked the idea at all. Knowing how my mother felt about drinking, Jim asked her for advice.

"Well, Jim, you need a part-time job," was her matter-of-fact reply. "A job is a job, and I think you ought to take it."

The new job paid a dollar twenty five an hour at Shakey's Pizza Parlor. Pizza was a new product in the Northwest and the restaurant where Jim worked was only the second Shakey's to open in what would one day become a chain.

I discovered I was pregnant shortly after Jim started at Shakey's. The doctors gave us little encouragement, recommending only that we take the baby early by Caesarean and that we anticipate special treatment which would cost a great deal. We tried to prepare for the expenses. I was still in the plastics and toy business and concentrated on doing all I could to increase our income during the few months remaining. I did well, earning six times as much in the short selling season before Christmas as I would have made at my old job.

The medical expenses would take all of our savings, but Jim and I both felt we were doing the right thing, that we were at peace with God, and that we would be bringing someone special into the world. And that is what happened.

David was born prematurely on December 10th, 1957. I was awake during the Caesarean delivery and heard his first cry, but didn't get to see him. They whisked him away for a complete blood change and he went directly into an incubator in the nursery.

Two days later the doctors told us there was no hope, that his little lungs had collapsed, and that he was in need of yet another blood change. We were also warned that, should he survive, the special treatment he had received might result in retardation or blindness. Only a miracle could save him.

Everyone, including Mom, encouraged me to give him up and an Episcopal priest offered to baptize him. This happened at a time when mothers were confined to bed several days after a delivery, especially a Caesarean one, and I still hadn't seen David. I had to be near him. I got up and went to the nursery in a wheelchair.

David looked so small in the incubator, struggling for every breath. No one could touch or cuddle him, except with gloves through access ports, and I made up my mind not to give up as long as he worked so hard to stay alive. I turned to the priest and told him David would be baptized when he got home.

Dad Covalt came to visit and found me sobbing.

"Stop crying, Iz," he told me, "and turn that energy to prayer."

I did, and so did many others.

My doctor came in the next morning to announce a change in David's condition. He seemed puzzled.

"I don't know what happened," he said, "but he is not only alive, he is slightly better than he was yesterday. It's a miracle." The doctors said they had only seen one other such case survive. David improved a little more each day and we took him home on Christmas eve.

Christmas eve, 1957. Baby David in Izzy's lap, just home from the hospital, with Jimmy and Freddy on the left, and Patti on the right.

We now had four children, and David was home safe. We had a wonderful Christmas that year. I thought of how alone David must have felt in that incubator and believed his spirit was affected by it. I saw a detachment, a kind of wall he protectively erected around himself. I'd never seen this in my other babies. I believed David had a special mission in life, a special reason for having survived.

I monitored David's every move for six months. Despite the doctor's gloomy predictions that he would not be normal, he developed on or ahead of schedule in every way. When I became comfortable that David was going to be fine, physically and mentally, I shifted my focus to Jimmy's progress. He was two-and-a-half years old and still not talking. I kept my concerns to myself, unable to face the possibility that Jimmy might not be developing mentally.

When I finally braced myself to raise such a painful prospect to Big Jim, I was relieved by his reassurance that Jimmy would be fine. After all, his optimism had pulled us through many times in the past.

Over the next few months, I continued to watch Jimmy anxiously, looking for signs of progress. Finally, my friend Helen O'Connor confronted me and said, "Izzy, something's not right with Jimmy. Get him to a doctor."

The doctors at the medical school confirmed my fears. Jimmy's mental development was well below average. They offered no suggestions or hope. I was devastated. Jim, on the other hand, insisted that Jimmy was not mentally deficient, citing sources he had studied in college psychology classes. He continued to encourage me not to give up.

One day, several months following the diagnosis, Jim raised his voice while talking to Jimmy to get his attention, but Jimmy still didn't react. He was looking at me when I repeated what his father had said and he responded immediately.

"Jim," I exclaimed, "I don't think he can hear you!"

We tested him by covering our mouths when we talked and discovered he had been lip reading. Our pediatrician confirmed it. Jimmy was deaf.

We were referred to a hearing specialist who determined the deafness was caused by swelling in his inner ears. He recommended we have Jimmy's tonsils and adenoids removed, which we did. Jimmy's apparent high tolerance for pain caught us by surprise. He had always seemed to be so happy and easy going, we never knew that he was having what must have been painful ear infections. It was unbelievable how fast Jimmy learned after the operation. By the time he was four-and-a-half years old he caught up with everyone and was ready for pre-kindergarten.

Throughout these difficult times, Patti continued to flourish and was a big help to me. My friendship with Patti had developed early and I viewed her with awe from the beginning. Strong and beautiful, with large hazel eyes and a full face, her complexion had an olive tinge. She always seemed to be happy, calm, and reasonable, and solved her problems that way. She developed and did everything ahead of schedule. A high achiever, she was finishing up second grade when David was born. Personable, responsible, capable, helpful and happy Patti: everyone loved her!

Freddy was always more intense than Patti and still is. Life was not easy for him. He had difficulty sitting still, sleeping, and staying focused on a task. Yet he was exceptionally bright. We had him tested at the suggestion of a concerned teacher and found he was bored and unchallenged with kindergarten. Going to school wasn't a pleasant experience for him. We couldn't afford to put him in a special accelerated program and he often cried when we insisted he go to public school. I talked to his teacher and principal about this, but their answer was always the same. He must attend school.

He enjoyed playing arithmetic "numbers" games with us at home and we were quick to participate when we discovered it challenged him. Later, when he entered first grade, things improved. His teacher recognized his special need and gave him extra work when he had time on his hands. He did well and she told us he showed leadership ability and helped other children with their work. We were relieved.

At last, all four kids were doing well, and we were managing financially. I was eager to see Jim graduate. We hoped he would get a job teaching in a rural area where I could open a little country store. Our dreams were within reach.

And then Jim changed the dream.

Chapter 9

Jim's enthusiasm for his part-time job at Shakey's Pizza Parlor surprised me. Each night, he returned home loaded with the pizza that had either been burned or dropped on the floor. It was always past midnight when he came home, and I woke up to the aroma of pizza in the room. While I sat in bed and munched, Jim gave me a full report on the number of pizzas that had been sold that night.

Jim and I discussed his interest in this pizza business. He wanted us to open a restaurant of our own, but cooking for a living was the last thing I wanted to do. I had never heard of pizza and thought it might only be a fad. Besides, he was always talking about some new interest or idea. But this time he persisted.

Our original goal of Jim's graduating and becoming a teacher seemed within reach. I had spent too many late nights typing Jim's papers and correcting his spelling to want to switch to another dream. I didn't know anything about restaurants, and even though we had all learned to love pizza when Jim started bringing leftovers home, I questioned whether it would capture a permanent place in the market.

When Jim met Shakey at work one night and asked him about the possibility of our buying a franchise, Shakey's reply was, "What's a franchise?" He had started his first pizza restaurant in Sacramento in 1954 and opened the second one in Portland in 1956, about nine months before Jim began tending bar. By the time Jim began working there, Shakey's was being advertised widely on Portland radio and was becoming well known. Pizza was new and different, and Shakey's was suddenly Portland's "in" place to be. The business was growing rapidly. I saw this happening, and I also became enthused about the franchise idea.

Mamita, Jim's stepmother, had often told Jim she would offer financial assistance to him if he ever wanted to go into business. We counted on this, and the discussions with Shakey became more serious.

Rod and Marty Tripp from Albany, Oregon, were regular customers at Shakey's, and Jim got to know them and their friends.

Rod was a realtor, and when he discovered Jim was interested in his own pizza restaurant, he encouraged him to consider Albany.

"Portland is too far for us to drive, Jim. We need a Shakey's of our own," Rod said.

Thus, the Tripps, too, became an important factor in our decision. They offered to build to suit on one of their key locations. This was just the first of many ways they encouraged us both as friends and business associates. Years later, it occurred to me that Rod had not even asked for a financial statement before building that first building. When I asked him about it, he replied, "I liked you both so much, I was afraid to ask."

It was beginning to look as if we were going to have a pizza business of our own. Shakey drove to Albany with us one day to look over a potential site. We contacted a lawyer to advise us in legal matters. Shakey predicted our start-up costs to be about twenty thousand dollars, of which five thousand needed to be in cash.

When everything was ready, we presented our business plan to Jim's parents and asked for the five thousand dollars. We were scheduled to meet with Shakey again in a few days to sign a franchise agreement that would include Albany, Corvallis, Eugene, and Salem. Mamita questioned us at length about the plan. We thought it was a great opportunity and were surprised when she didn't seem interested. She suggested we ask my parents for the money.

Jim was embarrassed and hurt. Mamita's unexpected change in attitude was frustrating. We had little time because we had to have the money in the bank before we could sign an agreement with Shakey. We left for Washington immediately, stopping first at Pete and Bunny's to tell them what was happening. They offered to borrow twenty-five-hundred at their bank and pass the four percent interest rate to us.

We drove on to the farm that night to talk to Daddy about getting the rest. I knew I could count on Mom to help persuade him, if needed. Daddy listened to the entire plan without comment. When I finished talking, he looked at me and said, "I'll go to the bank in the morning." Jim and I returned home, shaken but excited at our new prospect.

We signed the agreement with Shakey on August 18, 1958. It was the first franchise Shakey sold and was the beginning of what would soon become a large nationwide chain. That first franchise, which cost us three hundred dollars, in today's market would cost $100,000.

Within months, Seattle was franchised to Tommy Martin and we gave up Eugene to Cliff Magnuson. Cliff and Benny Brostoff began as partners in Eugene, but Benny eventually broke away to start "Red Lion Pizza" in 1961. Other competition wasn't long in coming. "Pietro's" was started in 1959 by some people in Longview who couldn't come to an agreement with Shakey.

It was becoming clear to many that pizza was in demand and was beginning to carve out a niche in the restaurant world. No one knew if

Izzy's parents, Fritz and Neldia Muenscher, in front of their home, 1961.

it would last, but we were getting in on the ground floor and were too busy to worry about it. Portland Shakey's was breaking previous sales records almost daily.

I resigned from the party business and became so involved in planning and building that I was unable to be with Bunny when she gave birth to William Peter Zuidmeer. Little Bill was the first Muenscher boy cousin and he and David were destined to become good friends.

Our building in Albany was the first to be built from the ground up specifically for a Shakey's Pizza Parlor. Shakey and Jim sketched it out together one night on a napkin, and we signed a twenty-year lease with Rod Tripp.

The necessary restaurant equipment was ordered from Kalberer's, a hotel and restaurant supply business in Portland. Kalberer's agreed to carry the ten thousand dollar purchase on a contract. We bought our neon sign the same way.

Gil DeSilva, manager of the Portland Shakey's, was to provide us with training and encouragement. Shakey's policy at the time was to hire only men, but there was one woman, Amy, working there at the time. She and Gil taught me the intricacies of pizza making. Shakey designed our pre-opening schedule and sat down with us to brainstorm ideas while I took notes. These notes became our operations manual.

On one of our visits to Albany with Shakey before we ever opened, we stopped at a restaurant for dinner. Shakey ordered a Martini and I decided to have one too. It went down easily and made me feel warm, energetic, and sure of myself. My anxiety about the risk we were taking disappeared. I liked this new setting of having a drink while discussing business. I felt confident. In fact, I was euphoric. For awhile, I forgot about my parenting responsibilities, Jim's blood pressure and weight which was a constant concern for both of us, the pain of estrangement from my cousins and friends as a result of the divorce, and the threat of Al taking custody of Patti and Freddy.

Martinis became my favorite out-to-dinner drink, but Jim and I didn't keep nor serve alcohol in our home—not yet.

Jim and I commuted to Albany frequently and were busy beyond belief. In a period of a few short weeks we hired a full-time live-in housekeeper, hired and trained employees, continued to check on construction progress and hired a CPA firm in Albany to set up our books. We put the Portland house up for sale and found a big old two-story house to rent in Albany.

We couldn't move until the last minute for two reasons: one, we needed to absorb as much training at the Portland Shakey's as possible, and two, our finances were stretched so thin that we needed Jim's bartending income to meet daily demands. Fortunately, the Portland house sold soon after the move and provided a small financial cushion.

Jim worked in Portland until June 9th. We loaded the car and a

U-Haul truck after he got off work that night and made the move. There was no turning back.

When it came time for the grand opening, ten days later on June 19th, we were ready. Gil DeSilva brought a crew from Portland to help with the opening and stayed with us that first week. Rod and Marty Tripp must have invited everyone they knew to come as their guest at some point during our first month of business, and the place was full the first night we opened.

I remember the let-down after that first night. We had worked months getting ready and it seemed that after the hectic pace of the evening and all the cleanup that followed, we had really accomplished something. "Whew!" I said to Jim as we left, "I'm glad that's over." He just laughed and said, "That's only the beginning, Iz."

To build the business, we knew we needed to be open every night. There were many nights, however, when there were few customers. We couldn't afford to hire help for those nights, and naturally we had to be there on the busy weekends, so Jim and I worked seven days a week. Jim tended bar and worked the tables while I handled the kitchen.

At that time, Shakey's pizza dough was made by a Portland bakery from a secret recipe. We sent an employee every two days to pick it up. The dough would raise during the return trip and the plastic bags containing it would sometimes pop if someone didn't stop to relieve the pressure in the bags. Jim later developed our own mix and we contracted with a bakery in nearby Lebanon to produce it. This eliminated the long and costly trips to Portland.

I did the payroll every Saturday night so that employees could pick up their checks after closing. Jim and I spent many late nights coordinating our thoughts to ensure that we were united in management decisions. We always deferred decisions deviating from policy until we could talk about it privately. I believe our employees saw this and respected us for it. We knew employee loyalty depended on not only setting rules, but also leading by example, and so we always paid for anything we ate or drank and saw that it was rung up on the cash register. This applied to our kids as well.

Although we served beer and wine, neither Jim nor I drank alcoholic beverages on the premises. This rule is still in effect in our restaurants today, and was broken by me only for a few short months, years later.

Before we opened, I had calculated that our break-even point was five thousand dollars a month in sales, and my projections proved to be accurate. Of the five thousand dollars, thirty percent went to food, twenty percent to labor, another twenty percent to operating expenses, and ten percent to fixed expenses. Of the remaining twenty percent, we decided to use only four hundred dollars to live on. We put the rest into a reserve fund.

We also had to pay interest on the loans from my family, due each February and August. The financial assistance we had received from them was a once-in-a-lifetime thing, and we knew it. We had to be successful!

Jim and I worked hard and only dropped below our break-even point one month. Having sales of only forty-nine-hundred dollars was terrifying to me. For all I knew, this could be the beginning of the end. I trimmed labor costs by closely analyzing sales trends and adjusting the staff schedule accordingly.

Jim and I found that our skills blended well, and business flourished as a result. Jim had the vision, faith and attitude to keep us in balance. I had the business training learned from Daddy and my ability to budget, schedule, and set the pace. Together, we made it happen.

Our teamwork and balance carried over into our home life. We each did what we liked best, and together, we seemed to cover all the bases. While we both worked long hours, we took turns slipping away for an hour or two to be attentive to the kids' needs, whatever they might be.

I had been afraid that pulling Patti and Freddy away from their Portland friends would be difficult, but they adjusted quickly. They did a lot of reading that summer and improved their skills noticeably. It was exciting to see Freddy begin reading for pleasure. Finally able to afford it, we enrolled both Patti and Freddy in a community swimming program at the city pool only a few blocks from our home and they soon became excellent swimmers.

In August, my baby sister, Elinor, now twenty, was married. She and Lonnie Montgomery had been high school sweethearts. He was competent and responsible and good to our sweet, gentle Elinor. And she was good to him.

Everyone was delighted. Jim and I loaded the car with kids and pizza for our first weekend off since the opening in June and headed for Bellingham.

It was a beautiful weekend and a beautiful wedding. Elinor was a tall, slender, elegant bride, and she seemed so happy.

When school started that fall, I became involved with the PTA, and when Freddy couldn't find a vacancy in Cub Scouts, I became a den mother. On a rare day that I was home, Kitty Fisher knocked on my door. We had met at a PTA function. She offered to be my Cub Scout den assistant if her son Bill could become part of the group. I was delighted to have some help.

Later, Kitty invited me to be a guest at an Altrusa meeting. Altrusa is the pioneer of women's service clubs, organized in 1917. I became a member and later served a term as president. Our first Altrusa Pizza Party was initiated in 1962, in which Jim and I turned over all the profits of our Albany restaurant for one day to Altrusa. This has continued for more than thirty years and was later duplicated by our restaurants in Corvallis and Eugene. I continued actively with Altrusa for about ten years.

Because I felt that church attendance was important for the children, we attended the Lutheran church in Albany. When Jim and I had worked especially late the night before, members of the congregation picked up Patti, Freddy, and sometimes Jimmy for Sunday school. I was grateful to them for their dedication.

Patti, Freddy, Jimmy, and David seemed happy and were doing well, and then something happened that startled me. Our live-in housekeeper was shocked one evening when I announced we were taking the entire family to the Tripp's home for dinner.

"Not David!" she exclaimed.

I hadn't realized how attached she had become to my baby boy. Her intensity scared me. Starting the business had taken so much of our concentration and time, but we were now doing well enough. I vowed to take more time off just to be with the children. Weekends were impossible at first, but we gradually became able to free ourselves for a Monday or Tuesday at the coast, even though it meant taking the kids out of school. Later, Jim and I found time for the two of us to get away together.

Jim and I visited the original Shakey's in Sacramento in 1960. We met with Shakey and with Ed Plummer while we were there. Ed was Shakey's partner and financial planner. It was soon evident that Shakey's role was to create and promote. We talked to them about opening a restaurant in Corvallis, the home of Oregon State University. The idea of opening a Shakey's on a college campus where we wouldn't be able to serve alcohol was a first. We also wanted a remodel to avoid the time-consuming expense of a custom building. Shakey agreed and we returned to Oregon to find a small location that was easy to put together.

In the meantime, our life took another turn. Our friends, Ross McCormick, an attorney, and his wife Nancy visited us one evening. Ross mentioned one of his clients, who was about to give birth. He hadn't been able to find suitable adoptive parents. He talked to us about his concern. Jim and I discussed this after the McCormicks left, and agreed we wanted to know more about the baby.

I had had my tubes tied after David was born so that we wouldn't be tempted to risk another pregnancy. The more we thought about it, the more we realized how fortunate we would be if we could adopt this baby. I thanked God for this opportunity. Ross drew up the papers, we signed them, and he called us in just a few days to tell us we were the parents of a baby girl. We named her Lois Jane, after Jim's natural mother and my middle name.

Lois was three days old when we brought her home. I was surprised at how natural it felt when she was placed in my arms. I had expected her to feel like "someone else's baby," but I knew immediately that she was mine. I looked at her curly light hair and delicate features and couldn't wait to get her home where I could look at her and hold her.

Jim and I set up the basket for her in our room and I arranged to take several days off. I didn't want to leave her. In fact, I barely left the bedroom those first few days. I seemed to be reacting, physically, as if I had given birth to her myself.

I was amazed by the intensity of Jim's and my feeling for this baby girl. Jim now had a daughter of his very own, and he doted on her.

The State Children's Services Division didn't approve the adoption until after Lois Jane came to us. This was stressful for awhile, but our adoption was finally approved and we were relieved.

Patti, now eleven, proudly took charge of her new baby sister at every opportunity. Freddy helped out by shoveling sawdust for our home's burner all winter, a big job for a little boy. He also played on the Little League team Shakey's sponsored that first year. It was the first of many teams we sponsored in Albany over the years.

Coinciding with Lois Jane's arrival and our work on getting the Corvallis campus restaurant ready, was the opening of my brother, Fred's, own Shakey's franchise in Bellingham in early July. Fred had been interested in our business almost from the beginning. He had majored in business at Pacific Lutheran College and served two years in the Army where he met and married Esther, a girl from Houston, Texas. Since his discharge, he had taken over the farm in Ten Mile, and Daddy had retired. In 1960, Fred decided to form a partnership with Ed Chasteen and bought a Shakey's franchise for Bellingham, Washington. Daddy supported Fred in this move and they sold the herd.

Ed was a boyhood friend from Ten Mile, and he and Fred trained with us in Albany while their restaurant was being built. Since Lois Jane was only a few days old when they opened, I stayed home with the family while Jim went to Bellingham to help out. Like ours, the Bellingham Shakey's was an instant success. Washington State, unlike Oregon, permitted live music with a beer and wine license, and they were filled beyond capacity on Friday and Saturday nights. Fred ran the bar and Ed ran the kitchen. They opened a second Shakey's in Everett in 1964.

Fred and Ed's partnership lasted for ten years and was just the beginning of Fred's success. By the mid-seventies, he was running close to twenty businesses, including other full-line restaurants, handball courts, and a golf course. He also bought the old Hinotes Corner at Ten Mile and expanded it into a grocery, floral, and hardware store.

In September of 1960, Mom came to see our new baby, Lois Jane, and to attend the opening of our Corvallis restaurant. Her visit was cut short when she received word that Grandma had died. Grandma was eighty-four and had been suffering from lung cancer. Grandpa had died the year before at eighty-seven. Both had enjoyed long healthy lives. I was sad to lose Grandma, but selfishly, I was disappointed to have Mom leave for the funeral just as we were opening in Corvallis. I was feeling a little guilty that I wasn't going with her, but Mom assured us she had plenty of support at home and returned to Bellingham, leaving us to attend to the family and the opening of the Corvallis "Pizza Pantry."

The addition of another restaurant proved to be more difficult than I had expected. Since we didn't have the space to store more than a day's supply of food in the new location, it was prepared in Albany and delivered daily. We did the accounting in Albany. It took all of our concentration in the fall of 1960 to manage this dual operation, so I was surprised and overwhelmed when Jim soon became interested in opening another location in Salem. He spent a lot of time looking for a suitable site and finally found one through Ben Higashi, who agreed to build to suit. After several months of construction, which Jim actively supervised, we opened our third Shakey's in north Salem in April of 1961.

But this new venture took its toll on my emotional well-being. Even though the business growth was both exciting and positive, I pushed myself to capacity, or beyond, daily. I resented Jim for leaving me to handle the hectic part of daily operations while he focused on the future. I often felt that I would no more get things settled down, then Jim would have another plan waiting to be launched. Just before the opening of the Salem restaurant in April, 1961, I'd had enough. I walked into the living room, pulled the drapes shut, and sat down in the darkness. Jim seemed to think I just needed quiet time and brought me something to eat, which I refused. Five children and the prospect of even more work for the restaurants just seemed too much. Possibly this was my way of saying to Jim: "Enough." I felt totally alone and isolated, even from Jim. I wanted to run away from everything: the pizza business, kids, Jim, responsibility. I suppose somewhere inside me, I knew I wouldn't do this, so I simply closed down. I just sat in my darkened living room, doing absolutely nothing.

After a few days, Jim knew my state of mind was different from my usual quiet breaks. He convinced me to seek outside help. I admitted I needed help and called a psychiatrist. During my sessions with Dr. Kimball, we discussed my workload, relationship to Jim and the children, and how to cope with stress. At this time, I was neither drinking nor taking drugs. He prescribed mood elevators for me and advised me to open up and talk more, especially to Jim, when things bothered me. He helped me to appreciate Jim for who he was, instead of my resenting him for doing what he did best. This awareness on my part helped our relationship considerably.

During this difficult time Jim quietly took care of the business as well as the children. I don't believe the kids even knew I was in crisis. Jim's support and the doctor's help allowed me to face the opening of the Salem restaurant with more positive feelings than I had thought possible.

This new enterprise was an instant success. By now, people in Salem knew about our Albany restaurant and were driving to Albany for pizza. On opening day in Salem, they lined up at the door, waiting to get in. The building was beautiful, and Jim had everything ready with time to spare, but the kitchen was equipped with the old Vulcan ovens which take two hours or so to heat up. We were scheduled to open at five o'clock, and I discovered too late that Jim had forgotten to turn the ovens on. The swarms of customers either waited until seven for their pizza or gave up and went home. It was frustrating, especially after all the careful planning Jim had done, but we were soon swamped with orders and profits rolled in. We sold five hundred pizzas the second night. We had transferred our Corvallis manager to Salem and we were grateful for his experience in this busy setting.

We now had three restaurants open seven-days-a-week. This third one had been Jim's dream, but now that it was open, Jim and I shared the responsibility in running it, and thanks to some better coping skills, I was able to do so energetically and with pride.

With three locations, we were forced to give more responsibility to each individual manager and Jim and I did more supervision. We took turns with frequent meal time visits, both scheduled and unscheduled. Sometimes we went together.

We held our first family picnic for the staff that summer of 1961. We picked a mid-week day because we didn't open the restaurants until four in the afternoon. There was lots of food and a keg of beer. Bunny and I worked all morning making tubs of potato salad and our friend and new landlord, Ben Higashi, brought huge stocks of bananas from his produce business. Everyone came: employees and their families, suppliers, landlords, friends and family. We played games and celebrated our successes together for the first time.

That fall Jim and I bought a comfortable three-bedroom house with a big yard and lots of nearby empty fields for the kids. The garage was remodeled into a large bedroom for the three boys. Because of their difference in age, Patti and Lois each had a room of their own.

I wanted Patti to have similar experiences with me to those I had with Daddy growing up with horses. We bought two and rented a barn for them. I tried to break them, as I had learned to do with Daddy so many years before, but it didn't go well. The oldest one, a mare, was unreliable. She was beautiful and had a smooth gait, but the professional trainer I eventually hired said she could never be trusted. He finally bought both of them from us. I had imagined it all so differently. Patti had already earned and bought her own saddle, and we were both disappointed in the way things turned out. Our riding from then on was done at Indian Ford Ranch near Sisters, Oregon.

In just under two years, we'd moved to a new community, added a fifth child to our family, and opened three restaurants.

The pace was exhausting, but exhilarating, and I had the satisfaction of knowing that, together, Jim and I were creating a good life for our children and for ourselves. At times, I was torn, worrying that I should be home with David and Lois Jane. I felt that they needed more time with Jim or me. Once, I even tried staying home, but it only lasted a few days. I became so anxious about the business and the decisions that needed to be made, that I knew I wanted to go back to work.

I comforted myself with the knowledge that while I was not being a traditional mother, Jim was not the traditional dad. He was actively involved with every aspect of the children's lives on a daily basis. He thrived on handling most of the homework, transportation, and school activities.

At last, I was coming closer to the balance of work and family I had craved for so long.

Izzy and Big Jim at work with David. North Salem Shakey's, 1962.

Big Jim Covalt and Izzy in their office, 1963.

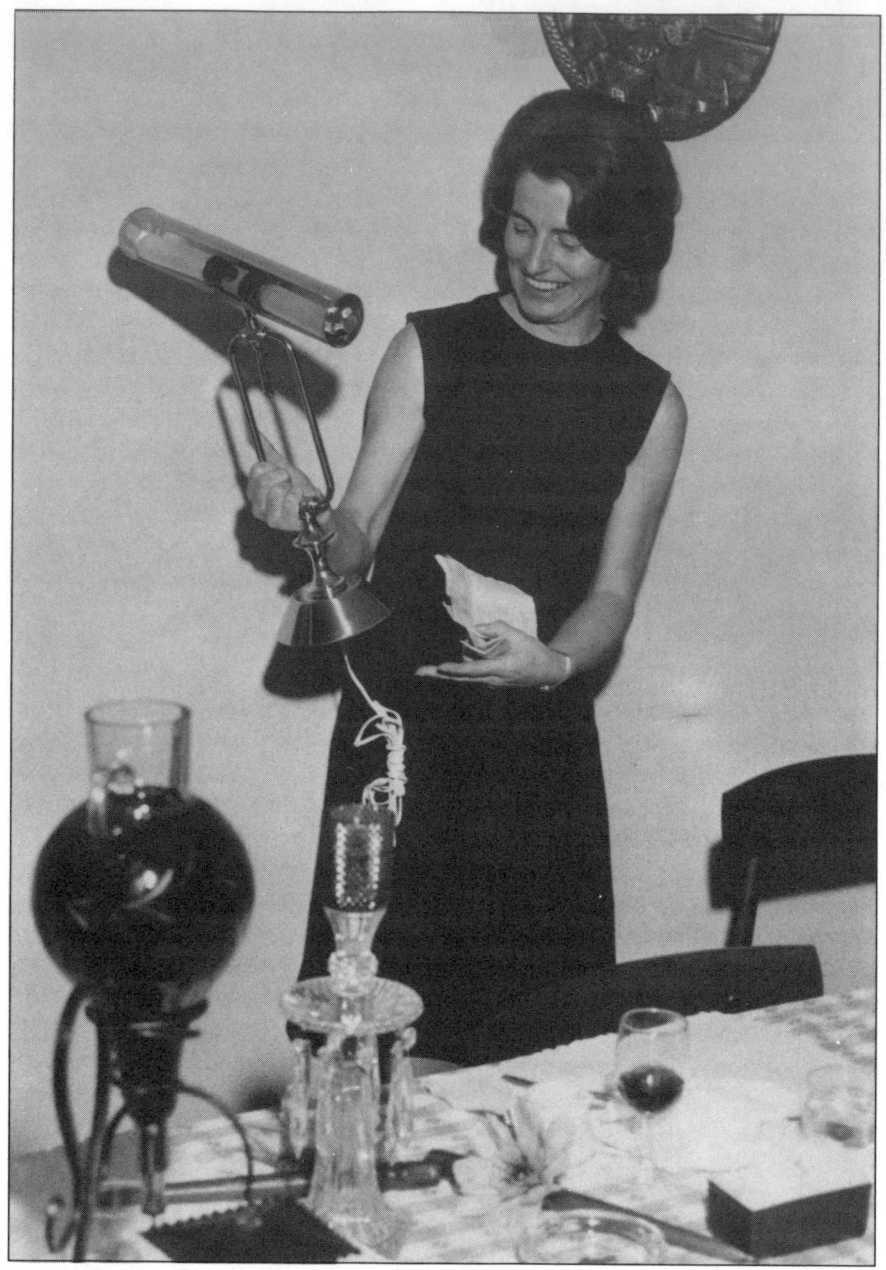

Izzy at her retirement as President of Altrusa Club of Albany, 1965.

A typical quality control visit at the Albany Shakey's, 1963. Jimmy, Big Jim, Lois Jane, and Izzy.

Chapter 10

By 1962, our business was continuing to grow at a breathtaking pace, breaking previous sales records nearly every day. No one knew when it would peak, but the enormous potential was so obvious we decided to take advantage of it. When Jim asked me about expanding again, I got caught up in his enthusiasm. Shakey told us he had sold all his nearby franchise areas, but offered us our choice of what remained, Alaska or Montana. His fee for either one would be one thousand dollars. We chose Montana.

Great Falls looked good. We found what appeared to be a good location and contracted with Tom Mather, a Great Falls realtor, to build for us. Then we offered Bunny and Pete a one-third working ownership.

It was a difficult move for Bunny. She was happy doing what she liked best, teaching home economics at Meridian High, but Pete's farming experience in Ten Mile had been disappointing. Bunny and Pete moved to Albany late that summer for training.

We opened in January, 1963. Shakey was there, but it was the last of our openings he attended. Most of his time would now be devoted to the chain's rapid expansion in Southern California and the escalating conflict developing within his partnership.

After the Great Falls opening, I took Mom, Freddy, who was twelve, and five-year-old David on a vacation to Mexico. My main purpose in taking this trip was that I was fairly convinced that Freddy, who was so compatible with me now, would soon lose interest in doing anything with me. I wanted to do one last thing with him before he went into his teens.

We flew first to Tucson to visit Jim's parents at their winter home, then traveled on to Mexico by train where we spent several days in the sun. It was a wonderful time. As it turned out, the break in our relationship which I had so dreaded never materialized. That "one last trip" has never ended.

While everything preceding the opening in Great Falls had gone according to plan, we found that establishing a business nearly a thousand miles away proved to be more difficult and time consuming than we had anticipated. Sales in Great Falls were low from the start.

Montana was a different kind of market. We weren't able to generate the excitement that attracted customers in Oregon. Bunny and Pete worked hard, but they were competing with a well known local pizza restaurant. It cost us about a thousand dollars a month to support Great Falls.

It was a stressful time for me; a thousand dollars was a huge drain on our resources. But Jim's optimistic reaction to this new source of worry was to want to open yet another restaurant in Salem. Before long he had found a promising location. This one in South Salem. I was dubious about this new venture but about this time a more personal opportunity turned my attention away from business.

Jim Wilson called me one morning as I was getting ready for work. A family friend and lawyer, he wanted us to look into adopting another baby. I reminded him of the five kids we already had, and tried to impress upon him that we didn't need any more, but he persisted. I'm glad he did.

He described the birth parents, suggesting the baby would probably be tall, and told me how well he thought the child would fit into our family.

"Let me discuss it with Jim," I said. "I'll call you back." Although my head said "no," I knew in my heart that we were meant to have this child.

Within three weeks we had another daughter, but not before we cleared the adoption with someone else: our housekeeper. Housekeepers had come and gone over the years. It had been difficult to find someone who would either go home or just disappear into the background when I came home from work to be with the children for an hour or two. Ruby Zink had come to us the year before. She seemed to have an innate understanding of our needs. Lois Jane had only recently grown out of diapers and we knew most of the added work would fall to Ms. Zink.

"Oh, Ms. Covalt, she said, "I don't know if I can start all over again, but I'll try."

As the due date approached, we made preparations for the baby's arrival. We put the basket in the bedroom and I made plans to take time off from work. When the due date came and went, and a couple of weeks had gone by, I found myself badgering the lawyer, asking for news.

Meanwhile, Jim made an important trip to Great Falls while I stayed home waiting for the baby to be born. At last, one Sunday morning, the lawyer called. The birth mother had been in labor fifteen hours and the baby could be born anytime.

The kids and I were expected in Portland that afternoon to pick up Jim from the airport. I made repeated calls for progress reports as the hours went by. Still no baby. Reluctantly, we left.

I began to worry about the baby's welfare after so long a labor. All sorts of things could be wrong, but there was nothing I could do but wait.

We picked up Jim on schedule and went to a restaurant for an early dinner. We knew we couldn't see the baby for three days, so there was no need to hurry home. But it was hard to think of anything else.

When everyone was seated at our table, I stepped out to the phone booth and made yet another call to see how things were going.

It was then that I learned we had a new baby girl. And she was fine.

Jim had already decided that her name would be Isabel Ann, but that we would call her Lis Ann.

Three days later, when our family doctor brought Lis Ann to us, Ms. Zink was there with the kids at the front door, just as eager to see the baby as the rest of the family. I gasped when I saw how beautiful Lis Ann was. For me, it was love at first sight. I reacted physically to Lis Ann's arrival as I had to Lois Jane's. Now that she was here, I was exhausted. I focused on settling down to spend a few days getting to know my baby.

A few months later Jim was on another trip to Great Falls when I received an emergency call at home. Our Corvallis manager wanted to close the Pizza Pantry temporarily in order to deal with a management crisis at Albany. The Albany restaurant was a much larger operation, generating far more revenue than the little Pizza Pantry, but we had always taken pride in how we ran our restaurants, opening on time and keeping posted hours. It was a difficult decision, but I agreed he was needed in Albany.

As I hung up the phone I discovered twelve-year-old Freddy had been listening to my side of the conversation.

"Mom, let me keep the Pantry open," he said eagerly.

"You don't even know how to make pizza, Freddy," I said.

"Yes, I do, Mom," he admitted somewhat sheepishly. "Leo taught me. I know we can do it if you'll help."

This was a revelation. Freddy had often helped in the restaurants, bussing tables or carrying out garbage, but he wasn't supposed to work in the kitchen. I paused, turning the idea over in my mind. I hadn't been in kitchen production for some time and knew I was out of touch, but we needed to stay open, and it might work.

"Okay," I said, noting his excited smile, "let's do it."

Patti took care of the kids, and Freddy and I kept Corvallis open until Leo was free to return. It was the first time Freddy had dealt with so much responsibility and he did a good job. The entire family was so proud of him that a subtle change occurred, seemingly overnight. Our Freddy became "Fred" from that day forward.

He approached us soon after this incident and asked to be baptized. He knew Patti had received the sacrament as an infant, as had many of his friends. His persistence inspired us to have Jimmy, David, Lois, and Lis Ann baptized as well.

Izzy with two-week-old Lis Ann with Lois Jane, 1963.

It was a family tradition that each child receive his or her godparents when baptized. Patti, Fred, and David had family members for godparents. Rod and Marty Tripp agreed to become Jimmy's, and our friends, Sandy and George Palmer, became Lois Jane's. Lis Ann's godparents were Kitty and Frank Fisher.

Eventually, David decided he wanted to ask my old friend, Jenny, and her husband Lowell Pollard to be his special godparents. Jenny had long ago divorced Bernie and married Lowell. They were homesteading in Alaska, but managed to visit us frequently. David loved them, and this further cemented their close relationship.

By the time we opened the South Salem restaurant on June 20, 1964, the other Oregon restaurants were doing well. We decided we needed an area supervisor and promoted our North Salem manager. We didn't have written guidelines for his position, but trusted his skill and experience to set his own schedule. This later proved to be a serious error and contributed to other factors that cost us thousands of dollars. South's initial sales were lower than we expected. Pietro's had opened in a superior location nearby just before we opened. At the same time, North Salem's sales began to decline as pizza customers found themselves with three options instead of one.

Then something unexpected happened that added to everyone's stress, affecting Jim most of all. His grandmother Covalt in Bellingham began suffering great pain and asked Jim for advice. She was eighty-six and her doctors recommended surgery, suspecting cancer. Jim urged her to have the operation.

As it turned out, it wasn't cancer, and the surgery hadn't been necessary. She died from surgical complications a few days later. Jim was heartbroken. He blamed himself for advising her and became depressed and withdrawn. I worried that part of his depression might be a symptom of his long-standing kidney problem. A physical examination showed that the condition had not worsened, so I suggested that Jim see Dr. Kimball, my psychiatrist. Even with this help, it took Jim several months to reconcile himself with his grandmother's death and to start functioning well again.

This left me solely responsible for keeping the family and all of the businesses going. In addition, we had already committed to two new projects: a new, full-sized restaurant in Corvallis on 9th Street, and a large office and commissary building in Albany. To add to the stress, Great Falls continued to lose money and Salem's reduced sales began to affect our cash flow. I was scared, and because I couldn't turn to either Jim or Bunny, I shared my concerns with brother Fred. He encouraged me to forge ahead and I did, but not without misgivings.

Fortunately, by the time construction started in Corvallis and Albany, Jim came out of his depression and became his old self again. With the stress eased, I took a short break and flew to Alaska to visit Lowell and Jenny at their lovely homestead on Eagle River. It seemed to me that, lately, crisis had followed crisis and I was relieved that we had managed to get through them thus far. The quiet beauty of the Alaska wilderness revitalized me and I returned home ready to forge ahead.

We were now busier than ever. We moved to a larger place on a lake which we were able to turn into a seven-bedroom home. It became a hub of activity for our family and friends. There was always at least one extra kid for dinner. Jim and the children did most of the grocery shopping around the menus I planned each week. We often bought food in bulk and the storeroom sometimes overflowed.

We continued sponsoring Little League baseball teams and I made Jimmy play on one of them. He was so sensitive and gentle I felt that sports would toughen him up and help prepare him for life. This brought me out to watch his games. One day he was put out by a third baseman.

"Why didn't you slide under him?" I admonished. "You might not have been put out."

"I didn't want to get my pants dirty."

"From now on," I said with emphasis, "you slide when you need to slide. Don't worry about your pants."

Jimmy never did became a great baseball player, but he did excel at football and wrestling later.

In the fall of 1964, I went to California. Jim and I had heard exciting stories about Shakey's expansion and wanted to see it first hand. When I learned that my brother Fred and his partner planned to visit Shakey's head offices in Burlingame, I decided to go with them. We had an appointment to see Shakey, but gave up after several hours of waiting.

Pete, Bunny, and Jim had had a similar experience a few weeks earlier, and we began to wonder at this uncharacteristic behavior. We later discovered Shakey and his partner, Ed Plummer, were fighting bitterly over corporate decisions. Shakey finally got out of the debate by selling his shares of stock for four million dollars. Ed continued holding his for several years, netting nine million when he finally sold.

The losses at Great Falls continued and began to create considerable emotional stress within our family. Brother Fred suggested that Pete and Bunny might do better independently and he helped them locate a site in Missoula with a franchise of their own. The arrangement worked well, and we were all pleased. Bunny went back to teaching while Pete managed the restaurant. We took over full responsibility for Great Falls, and hired a manager until we could decide what our next step should be.

In March of 1965, Mom and Daddy were celebrating Daddy's birthday in Albany with us when I received a call from the bank which spoiled their visit. We were overdrawn. I was sure the bank had made a mistake, but we investigated and found the manager of our South Salem restaurant hadn't been making deposits. Jim wanted to fire the young manager at once, but I knew him to be a bright and extremely capable person and pleaded with Jim to give him a second chance, believing he had learned his lesson. Six months and ten thousand dollars later, I realized I was wrong. We fired him and were going to prosecute, but in the courtroom it felt more like I was being prosecuted. I told Jim I didn't want to go through with the proceedings. Jim agreed; our ex-manager went his way, and we never heard from him again.

This betrayal of trust was a shock and disappointment to us, but we also realized our controls were too loose. Something had to be done, not only to prevent such things from happening in the future, but to improve our bookkeeping and accounting. The business had grown too big for us to manage like a mom-and-pop store, comfortable as that had been. The solution was really quite simple, and I am sorry we didn't see it sooner. It simply involved bringing in professional help.

We asked Don Brudvig, our Albany CPA, to update our systems and train me to manage them, which he did. One of our first steps was to increase the hours and responsibilities of Sandy Palmer, who had been working for us part-time for two or three years. Eventually, we added more office staff. With the embezzlement crisis over and the successful opening of the Corvallis restaurant, and our beautiful new office and commissary, we found ourselves wanting a break from routine. After considering the options we decided to take the entire family on a vacation for the first time. It almost worked. I chose Indian Ford Ranch. Our first hold-out was Fred who opted to take his vacation in Bellingham where he helped his uncle Fred in his restaurants. Everyone else was there at first, but after twenty-four hours it became evident Lis Ann wasn't ready for it. In spite of her charming smiles and beautiful dark eyes, her energy was too much to manage in such a public setting. Jim took her back to Ms. Zink. It was a wonderful experience for the rest of us, however. We ate ranch cuisine, rode horses, swam, and participated together in arts and crafts. I was especially proud of four-year-old Lois who took to the horses at Indian Ford as I had taken to Buster at the same age.

Lois was fine-boned with blue eyes and brown hair that curled naturally. She was quiet and a little shy. I had concerns about her sensitive nature and I was thrilled to see her confidence and sense of command on horseback.

Over the years, the kids and I returned many times to Indian Ford, usually for a few days, and often with relatives or friends of the children. The children stayed busy with all the ranch activities, so I was often free to ride the trails for extended periods. Being alone and on horseback, combined with the knowledge that my kids were nearby and happy, provided a freedom that was heavenly. Jim seldom went with us. Horses and ranching weren't his favorite things, but he often left the business to drive over to visit or to join us for dinner.

On one of our short visits I unexpectedly found myself employed there. Though a paying guest, I loved to get up early and hang around the barn, helping and talking with the wranglers. They got to know me and I was pleased when they began trusting me with the more spirited horses on trail rides.

One day I casually suggested they should call me if they ever needed an extra wrangler. Imagine my surprise a few hours later when the owner, Donna Gill, asked if I could start work the next day! My adrenalin began to build. I hadn't expected to be taken seriously, but it was a dream come true. My love of horses and the outdoors had led me to think often of having a ranching business of my own. They needed me for one whole week, and I thanked God for Jim and his understanding! It meant he would have to take all the responsibility at home as well as the business, but his response to my enthusiastic call was predictable.

"Sure, Iz, I'll pick up the kids tomorrow and work it out. It'll be fine."

And I started my new, albeit temporary, job. It meant I would be getting up early to be on the job at five, two hours earlier than I was used to, and moving my belongings from the guest house to the bunkhouse. I was a wrangler!

By the end of the week I was promoted to "Lead Wrangler" for a few rides. Jim's curiosity got the best of him and he arrived for a visit on my last day. He wasn't an experienced rider and I felt a sense of pride when they trusted me to take him out by myself.

Although Jim didn't spend much time at Indian Ford, he did have an annual outdoor vacation, camping with Rod Tripp and a group of friends on bow hunting expeditions to Eastern Oregon. He wasn't a hunter, but went along to fish and enjoy the fellowship. I took my turn to manage everything while he was gone.

I once found a wooded acreage for sale while he was away and bought it at a bargain price. Jim was naturally surprised when he came home, but he was also pleased. One thing led to another and real estate investing became a hobby for me.

The things that Jim and I did independently of one another never affected our unity in our business and family lives. Even though our activities might be very different, our goals were always shared. One of our goals was that our children should be kept busy and learn the value of hard work. For this reason, as each child reached the age of twelve, he or she got the "opportunity" to work for us.

Having the kids in the business not only helped them to learn to manage their own money, but it also gave them valuable business experience and kept them close to us. When we started an employee profit sharing plan and began investing in the stock market, we also purchased stock for the kids.

David's stock share prompted him to begin watching daily market reports and graphing them, but his stocks remained static for so long he lost interest. He was nine at the time. The experience, however, indicated to us that he had an analytical mind, and I began bringing home financial statements for him to study.

Fred also became interested and involved, and while my two "investors" eagerly constructed graphs and analyzed financial statements, Jimmy read history books and kept up on current events. Since this was something that had always interested his dad, the two had frequent animated discussions over the news or some political crisis.

I was still concerned about how Jimmy would cope as an adult with conflicts over which he had no control. He was so easy-going and happy, I couldn't see what might motivate him. He loved to read, but I worried that he didn't have enough drive to achieve his goals, whatever they might turn out to be. A friend with similar concerns about her son suggested we consider a military school. She had enrolled her son in such a school for one summer and felt the experience had helped him. It sounded like a good idea. Jimmy was continuing to have trouble with math, and a summer tutorial might help.

We sent him to a school in San Rafael, California, when he was eleven-years-old. He was homesick and called home frequently during the first weeks. Fearing he was leaning too much on me for emotional support, I suggested he limit his calls to Sunday afternoons. This regimen may or may not have helped Jimmy, but it made a nervous wreck out of me. Sunday finally came and he called to tell me he had gotten lost for awhile on a mountain hike. I suddenly felt sick.

"Weren't you scared?" I managed to ask.

"Yeah, Mom," he replied, "but I finally found my way back. The group leader was so mad he kicked me all the way to camp."

"That's awful! Why did he do that?"

"That wasn't the worst of it. When we got back, he made me run laps around the track as punishment." Jim and I discussed this incident at length. Could we trust the people at the school? Had we made a mistake in sending Jimmy? We eventually decided Jimmy should finish the six-week course. He went through other difficult times at the academy, and teases me about it today. "What are you going to do, Mom, send me back to San Rafael?" he chides when he thinks I'm coming on too strong.

Jimmy grew up to be a successful businessman and I'm not sure it was necessary to put him through such an experience. Whenever I look at him I still see that wonderful "gentle boy."

All six children, 1964. Jimmy, Lois Jane, Freddy, Lis Ann, Patti, and David. This portrait was arranged and organized as a surprise for Jim and Izzy by then fifteen-year-old Patti.

Chapter 11

Our rapid business expansion had proved wise, but the stress continued to keep us on edge. I wanted to relax a little and consolidate our resources before taking new risks. Not so with Jim. At my insistence, he stopped considering new restaurant locations. But then he proceeded to launch a home delivery system. His idea was to take a Volkswagen "Bug," cut the back out of it, and mount an oven over the engine.

Platt Davis of Albany had the technical skills to create the oven and a shop to fabricate the conversions. Another corporation was born. Before long, home delivery accounted for twenty-five percent of our business.

Jim and Platt put a lot of effort into perfecting and marketing the ovens and sold a few. They were attractive and drew a lot of attention. Nations Restaurant News did a feature story on the ovens and we switched to pickup trucks so we could market the ovens independently of the vehicle design. It was a new idea and we sold several ovens. Actually, they were too expensive and required too much maintenance to be practical, but it was an interesting adventure.

In 1967, a large business consulting firm contacted us with the suggestion that we participate in an efficiency audit. I didn't like the idea at first, but Jim was always thinking of better ways to do things and persuaded me to try it. It was a wise move. They helped us look at our strengths and weaknesses and recommended changes that were quite beneficial.

We developed precise job descriptions which, in turn, allowed us to define guidelines, create budgets, and set standards. From this we established an incentive plan to share our net profit with employees, resulting in increased productivity and even better relations. We changed our monthly staff meetings to twice-a-month, planning and forecasting sales at the first one, and reviewing results at the second.

This company taught us how to use screening and testing methods for evaluating management potential before hiring or promoting employees. These practices helped our area supervisors be more accountable and effective. Then we were shown how to make our inspections and evaluations more result-oriented. Efficiency soared and our work load eased further. It was money well spent.

I was living each day to the fullest, often combining family and business, but many times I came home exhausted. Jim usually sensed when I'd be spent after pushing hard all day at work and would meet me at the door in the evening with a glass of orange juice. It picked me up and helped me shift from business tasks to dinner preparation and our time with the kids.

Once in a while I required more than orange juice and let everyone know I needed quiet time, a retreat to my room. I liked to curl up with a book or watch T.V. whenever I needed this kind of respite. Sooner or later I would hear a knock at the door, someone bringing dinner in on a tray. I would then relax to the muffled music of busy family activities.

Most of the time, however, we maintained a regular family dinner hour, everyone coming to the table with clean faces, clean clothes. The children all had their own places, with Jim at one end and me at the other. Jim and I both felt we needed these gatherings because these were the only times we were all together. We had a moment of quiet before we prayed. This gathering made dinner the high point of the day.

Friday and Saturday were our busiest nights at the restaurants, but we managed to get away with the family occasionally, usually for a drive-in movie. We would load up the station wagon with kids, popcorn, and Kool-Aid to spend a few stress-free hours together. More often than not, I would choose to stay at home with just one of the children. When this happened, Jim, understanding of my idiosyncracies, would go to the store and return with lots of magazines and loads of treats for us to enjoy during our evening without the rest of the family.

When Patti graduated from high school in 1967, we hosted the senior party in our backyard. About one hundred seniors attended. The kids successfully handled discipline problems and everyone seemed to have a good time. We laughed, barbecued hamburgers, and swam in the lake.

This same summer Fred went to work for Al doing construction work in Alaska while Patti worked as a counselor at Camp Lutherwood east of Eugene. My kids were growing up. I wasn't ready for Patti and Fred to leave home. While I wanted what was best for them, it felt so final for me. I was going to have to let go and it scared me. I would no longer be in touch with them every day, and knew I had to trust them to make decisions based on their own knowledge and intuition.

I made several short trips home to the farm that summer. In his retirement, Daddy was raising beef cattle and horses. And, he was logging some of the wooded acreage. I enjoyed helping him with the chores when I visited, as I had as a girl. That August, I helped him prepare two teams for a draft horse pulling contest at the Whatcom County Fairgrounds. I had often dreamed of competing with one of the teams, but knew tradition barred women from the event. My brother Fred was expected to drive one team, Daddy, the second, and my satisfaction had to come from knowing I helped with the training. Daddy worked one team while I worked the other and I felt like a kid again. "Pat" and "Bolly" pulled well for me and I fantasized about something happening that would allow me to enter the competition. It wasn't to be. Fred showed up as planned and I reluctantly turned the team over to him. He never knew how much I had wanted to drive them, to see their beautiful muscular bodies respond to my commands.

After the summer break of 1967, my workload increased. I was satisfied with my work, but had difficulty relaxing and letting down. I also experienced shortness of breath and occasional hyperventilation. My psychiatrist described this as anxiety attacks and prescribed tranquilizers. We began to explore what was behind some of these symptoms.

I wasn't prepared for what we found. I learned that my attachment to Daddy had been unusually strong, and had to acknowledge my childhood fear of losing him to alcohol or some other mishap. I began to realize how much I lived for my children and was still living for Daddy, but the time had not yet come when I could live "just for me." It would take David's brush with death and losing Jim a few years later to bring about that change.

As my therapy continued, I found myself wanting more tranquilizers than my prescription allowed. I didn't tell Dr. Kimball, but discovered that a drink in the evening was an excellent substitute for a tranquilizer. Increasingly, I looked forward to these drinks. Like orange juice, alcohol readily eased the transition from my fast work pace to family activities, though in a vastly different way. While one glass of orange juice was more than adequate, I found that one glass of wine often led to a second. And, after the wine, I seldom had energy to do anything with the kids.

When Patti moved to Eugene to attend the University of Oregon that fall, I missed her. But I focused on the rest of the family and the beginning of their new school year. During this period Aunt Essie was diagnosed with cancer and she was rapidly failing. I visited her several times, and finally brought her to stay with us when I returned from a trip to Bellingham in 1968. It was only for a few weeks, but she seemed to enjoy the family and I installed a reclining chair for her in my office so that she could be with me during the day.

"Oh honey, I hate to leave you," she said as Mom and Daddy came for her. She died a month later.

During Aunt Essie's illness, I was also worried about my friend Kitty Fisher. She had undergone a radical mastectomy. The survival rate for Kitty's type of cancer wasn't very high in 1968. It has hard for me to watch her go through this difficult period, but I was determined to be there for her and her family.

Izzy and her dad preparing for a draft horse pulling contest, 1967.

I continued to struggle with my anxiety attacks. The problem became so severe that I usually refused to ride in a car with anyone other than Jim driving, and even then, I was less likely to have an attack if I drove. But we were often out with another couple. Before I could consider getting into a car with anyone else behind the wheel I would ask Jim to explain to them that they might need to pull over on short notice to let me out should I begin to hyperventilate.

Because this embarrassed me so much, we went to great lengths to avoid putting me in this situation. However, I knew I couldn't drink and drive, so if I wanted to drink somewhere other than at home, which I often did, I was automatically dependent on Jim, or someone, to drive.

The attacks increased in intensity and frequency. I sometimes needed to leave the office or get up from a luncheon meeting to walk around the block to bring my breathing back under control. And on more than one occasion I was so frightened, I asked Jim to take me to the emergency room. I went to my internist, who prescribed librium, and to Dr. Kimball, who increased my dosage of valium. Afraid to risk having my tranquilizer dosage reduced, I didn't tell either doctor about the other's prescriptions.

I frequently found myself visualizing Jenny's and Lowell's homestead in Alaska, which I had visited in 1964. Somehow, the image of that tranquil winding river, the serenity and the breathtaking color brought me peace.

I decided I needed to go there, and managed to get away for a brief visit after school started. I loved any time with Jenny and Lowell at their homestead, but this year the fall colors were spectacular. I returned home from Alaska, as I had before, refreshed and energized.

On June 19th, 1969, Jim and I celebrated our tenth anniversary in the restaurant business. Fred had recently graduated from high school and had already left to work full-time for Al in Alaska. I was devastated as my oldest boy left home. And I missed him at our celebration.

The day of festivities began when we met Shakey at the Salem airport with our fleet of pizza delivery vehicles. Our friend Rod Tripp brought his Rolls Royce and led the parade through Salem and down through Albany.

We took Shakey on a tour of each of our restaurants after which we had a formal banquet at the Marian Hotel in Salem. It was attended by our family, our closest friends, and our key employees. The alcohol flowed freely that night. For me, the party would not have been complete without it.

We were now doing so well that I no long worried about finances. This was quite a departure from the years of sacrifices and tight budgets. With this freedom came another awareness: alcohol was becoming more important to me.

Both Jim and I arranged our schedules to put us in the

restaurants several nights each week, sometimes singly, but often together. I found myself constantly trying to persuade him to stop after work for a drink. His response was nearly always negative. When he felt good, he didn't want to drink, and when he felt bad he thought it would make him feel worse. I didn't understand his attitude about alcohol. A drink always made me feel better, regardless of how I felt before I had it. I compensated for Jim's reluctance to stop after work by making sure we had an ample supply of alcohol at home. I found myself looking for any excuse to serve it.

By this time, I was having at least one or two drinks most evenings. This was awkward for Jim, who wasn't interested in drinking at home, either. To ensure that I wouldn't become an alcoholic, I established two rules. I made it a practice never to drink alone, and I wouldn't have a drink before five o'clock on a work day. I always started out believing I would only have one or two drinks, but I often had more and didn't always feel good the next day. Of course these "rules" only applied to working days, and even then, I didn't always keep them.

I found myself wanting to spend more time with people who drank like I did. I especially began to look forward to visits with Jim's sister Be, her husband, Dan, and her children. Be offered another excuse to "relax" with alcohol. She was a pleasant drinking companion, and our families often visited or went on trips together. We began seeing each other even more frequently when Dan's company transferred him to nearby Beaverton, Oregon.

Although our businesses were going well, we unfortunately found ourselves in a legal battle with Shakey's. Dissatisfaction among Shakey's franchisees had been increasing throughout the late sixties due to what was generally thought to be unfair charges for products. We were all obligated to buy certain products from them and the high prices made things very difficult for the newer franchisees. The conflict increased when it became apparent that Shakey's was indifferent to the complaints. Communication finally became so bad that we reluctantly joined other franchisees in a class action suit against the company. The franchisees won and the price of many products was reduced to true market value. After that, the relationship between Shakey's and the franchisees began to improve.

In the fall of 1969, Fred returned from Alaska to attend Willamette University. I was delighted to have him nearby and he came home several times a week. He played on the Willamette football team. It was a thrill to watch him. Everything seemed to be running smoothly when disaster struck from an entirely new direction.

The University of Oregon offered Patti the opportunity to join a world tour called Campus Afloat. The program offered full credit courses and she was excited about the ocean cruise. It was to be her junior year. Campus Afloat was expensive and impressed me as being frivolous, but I agreed when Patti won Jim's approval. Al, who had stayed close to Patti and Fred, agreed to pay half of the expenses for the trip, as he had shared equally in the cost of her college education thus far. Patti had developed a serious relationship with a Lane County Community College student named Bill. He seemed like a nice young man and was Patti's age, but appeared somewhat immature. He came to Portland with us to see her off on the voyage.

Her letters over the next months were regular, upbeat, and positive, and there was no hint of trouble until we received a telegram from the school. She was returning immediately. No reasons were given. We were extremely concerned. Abrupt changes in plans were not the kind of thing we had learned to expect from Patti.

She finally called and told us she had requested to be sent home. She was pregnant with Bill's baby and was planning to marry him. I wasn't prepared for this news and was shocked! My beautiful, responsible, mature daughter was now at a painful crossroads. There was no way her life could ever be the same and I couldn't protect her from this harsh reality.

She called Bill to pick her up at the Portland Airport and made arrangements to meet us in Eugene. I spent most of the night drinking and crying. I left for Eugene with Jim the next morning, covering my swollen face and reddened eyes with dark glasses. It was New Year's Eve.

Bill wanted her to have an abortion and told us of a place where she could get it. We insisted it must be both safe and legal, which meant going to Japan. Patti agreed at first, but immediately had second thoughts. We told them we felt abortion was Patti's decision, because it was her body, her baby. I knew she would live with this the rest of her life. Bill seemed indifferent, but consented to marry Patti when she decided to keep the baby.

We helped them settle into an apartment and gave them a car so that Bill could continue going to school. Their relationship was strained from the beginning, but Patti spoke both hopefully and fearfully of their future each time I saw her. We offered them financial help from time to time and tried to remain optimistic. Bill went to work for us in our commissary when we offered the job to him, but appeared withdrawn and sulky when I was around. He disappeared, along with the small amount of money they had saved, when Patti was seven months pregnant. He called a few weeks later to tell her he couldn't manage, that the marriage was over. Patti was devastated and moved home again. Sometimes, late at night during those last months before the baby was born, she would crawl into bed between Jim and me and cry.

Courtney Be, my first grandchild, was a gorgeous baby. The surge of love I felt when she arrived was similar to what I had felt when her mother was born. I was sad that no father was present to share our joy. Although Patti lived with us at home, she made it clear who was responsible for taking care of Courtney. It was going to be Patti, not me.

Patti's hopes were rekindled when Bill came back after Courtney was born, but it was only temporary and he left again, this time never to return. This put Patti through another painful time and she had trouble acknowledging that the relationship was over, but finally came to us and asked for help with a divorce.

The experience, difficult as it had been, transformed Patti and brought out her strengths. She moved to Bellingham, got a job, and took charge of her life with little or no help from anyone.

Back where she was born, and surrounded by relatives, Patti flourished.

Chapter 12

Jim and I attended many franchisee dealer's meetings which were held all over the country. After one of the earliest meetings in January 1971, Jim and I flew to Mexico for a vacation. Jenny and Lowell were wintering in Chapala and we joined them there for a week. Ms. Zink took care of getting David and Jimmy packed and on a plane so they could meet us, too.

It was a wonderful vacation, probably in part because I didn't drink very much. Unaware of their influence, during our time together Jenny and Lowell repeatedly voiced their concern about the increase in drinking amongst their retired friends in Chapala. Because of this, I was self-conscious about drinking in front of them. I viewed it as an accomplishment on my part that I could drink little and still enjoy myself so much.

On our return home, I again threw myself into work and enjoyed my days. We were free from financial worries, and good things were happening for the family.

Patti's life brightened a few months after she moved to Bellingham with her introduction to Frank Imhof, a young man who worked for Al. Frank had grown up on the Imhof dairy farm near Ferndale, Washington, and was from a family Daddy greatly respected. We recognized Frank's sincerity and warmth the moment we met him and were delighted to attend Patti and Frank's wedding in November. Frank adopted Courtney soon after.

We kept Courtney with us in Albany for a month while they went on their honeymoon, and Jim became "Bapa" and I became "Gaga" during her brief stay. The names stuck.

Our own "little girls," Lois and Lis Ann, often dressed alike, with Lois in blue and Lissie in red, but they were as different in personality and appearance as they could be. Lis Ann had some natural curl in her hair, big brown eyes, and always appeared to have a suntan. She was tall and slender for her age by the time she started school.

Lois had beautiful brown curly hair, blue eyes, and a petite build. Although three years older than Lis Ann, she wore the same size clothes. Where Lis Ann was bouncy, happy, and active, Lois was quiet and reserved. Lis Ann was easy going and never bore a grudge or pouted, while Lois seemed always intent about "getting things right." They were both gentle and loving. A delight to us all.

Meanwhile, Fred transferred to the business department at the University of Oregon. He seemed happy there and continued to work part-time to pay his way. David, too, was doing well. He was at Calapooia Junior High, excelling at everything, especially sports.

Although Jimmy wasn't as enthusiastic about sports as Fred or David, I always encouraged him to participate because he was such a natural athlete. He chose wrestling, and in this, his junior year, he placed second in the state tournament. It was a significant achievement for a junior in high school, and we were proud of him. His success made him more determined, so he set his sights on a first place finish for the following year. Unfortunately, he broke his wrist playing football the following fall and couldn't wrestle at all his senior year. But he followed the team closely. It must have been hard for him, watching the state finals from the bleachers, knowing that he had missed his chance.

Through all this, I continued to drink more and more. I drank even more heavily on weekends, and when evening meetings such as Altrusa interfered, I eventually quit attending. I also looked for excuses to start drinking before the normally acceptable cocktail hour after work.

Our Lutheran pastor must have sensed something was wrong when I stopped attending church or encouraging the children to go. He began visiting occasionally, usually on Sunday afternoons, and I was embarrassed to have him see empty beer cans lying around. I was relieved when he finally discontinued these visits. He had to have smelled the alcohol on my breath when I greeted him at the door.

My life finally narrowed to business commitments and the family. Alcohol gradually began to interfere with these as well.

In March, 1972 a tragedy occurred which deepened and further narrowed my perspective. I had taken David, Lis Ann, and Lois to Portland to visit Be while her husband Dan and son Danny went scuba diving near Port Angeles, Washington. Be and I went out to eat, leaving our children to enjoy one of Be's spaghetti and meatball dinners at home. I remember taking a cab in order not to have to worry about drinking and driving. We were sitting together over drinks when Dan's boss, Chuck, suddenly appeared at our table.

There had been an accident. Dan had drowned! Chuck had been with Dan and a group from work when the accident had happened. Somehow, he got us back to Be's house, where we could offer comfort to the kids who had heard the news before we got there. Dan left no will and I suddenly found myself the administrator of his estate. Be was devastated and I was barely able to cope.

There was substantial income from insurance, stock options with Dan's company, and Social Security. Be and the kids were therefore able to maintain their lifestyle, but Danny, Steve, and Kippy grieved so for their dad that I felt depressed beyond anything I had ever experienced.

Be and the children moved to Albany to be near us. We tried to help share the loss, but the tragedy and our closeness merely encouraged me to drink more. I began stopping at Be's for a drink on my way home nearly every evening throughout that summer and fall, and often failed to join my family in time for dinner.

When I didn't pass out at Be's and stay overnight, I would arrive home in no condition to do anything except fall into bed. This left Jim with more responsibility than ever. While he knew what I was doing, he never confronted me about it.

I began to realize that my drinking was out of control and it scared me. I had to drink. It was clearly no longer a social need, so I switched to drinking only beer, thinking I could drink more without getting drunk. With increased drinking came the return of a childhood scourge, bedwetting. I was appalled to wake up soaking wet as I had as a child.

For Lis Ann's birthday, on March 17, 1973, I managed to host an after-school birthday party for her, but all I could think about was ending the party so I could drink. As soon as everyone was gone I reached for my first beer, when I suddenly felt weak and shaky with chills. My fever rose so high that Jim took me to the emergency room at the hospital that evening. I had never experienced anything like this before. It turned out to be a kidney infection and my allergy to penicillin and sulfa prevented a quick cure. Fortunately, the doctors finally found a workable antibiotic.

The great fear haunting me during my recovery was that the doctors would find out I was an alcoholic and everyone, including my family, would learn about it. Finally, I turned to God and promised Him I would never drink again if He allowed me to survive the infection without anyone knowing. As I lay in bed, I reinforced my commitment not to drink. This decision strengthened me and I began to feel better about myself than I had for some time.

I felt guilty about how my increased drinking had affected the family and I resolved to make it up to them. I had put them through so much for more than a year. I was hospitalized for over a week and went home, thin, helpless, and again down to ninety-five pounds. Jim set up a hospital bed in our living room and Bunny came to stay until I could feed myself again.

I told Jim about my deal with God and my promise to not have alcohol, but didn't mention my fear of being branded an alcoholic. I felt we shouldn't let my resolve to not drink interfere with serving alcohol to others, and he honored my request. I didn't take another drink as long as Jim lived and we never talked about it again.

I believe my problem with hyperventilation had been aggravated by alcohol and my subsequent withdrawal from it, because the episodes decreased in frequency and intensity over the next couple of years, and I found that my need for prescription drugs also decreased.

While it took time for me to feel better physically, I noticed that without alcohol there was an immediate change in my focus. I became more aware and interested in those around me, and I looked forward to being strong enough to again become more involved in my childrens' lives.

The enforced bed rest allowed me to talk to Patti on the phone every day. Patti and Frank had moved to Moses Lake to work on a Jansen Construction Company project and were expecting a baby. It seemed interesting that she waited out the final days of her pregnancy in the same little town where I had given birth to her brother twenty-two years earlier.

She was a great support to me as I recuperated from the double burden of the infection and withdrawal from alcohol. Heather Jane Imhof was born on May 4th, 1973, a strong and energetic baby, but it was another month before I was well enough to travel to Moses Lake to see her.

During my illness, the business responsibilities had continued unabated. I normally met with each manager to go over monthly cost reviews at his respective restaurant, but for two months I was forced to conduct these meetings from the hospital bed in our living room with plenty of time to rest between sessions.

I did rest, and spent a lot of my time reflecting on each member of the family as I lay there. How could I do more for them, encourage them, help them raise their own expectations?

I had become particularly concerned about Lois Jane during my illness. She seemed moody and overly quiet. She spent more and more time alone in her room away from the family. I knew she loved animals, especially horses, and I determined to do something about it when I recovered.

Lois was thirteen now and had shown strong natural riding skills on our numerous trips to Indian Ford. She seemed capable, and I felt a horse would reinforce her dependability and good grades at school. I told Jim it was time to start looking and he agreed. By June 28th, Lois Jane's birthday, I was up and about sufficiently to accompany her. It reminded me of those delightful days so many years before when Daddy took me on the same quest. We found "Mac" for her the very first day!

The next step was to find a place to board him. Lois was soon enjoying many wonderful days riding and learning to work her horse. The pasture and riding area were several miles east of Albany. Lois Jane's transportation there and back became a factor in everyday activities. It was an added chore for me, but it never appeared to burden her dad. Jim picked her up and was patient and loving with her, as always. He never played favorites with the kids and they all knew he loved them, but there was something unique in his relationship with Lois Jane from the beginning, a distinct closeness. He seemed to be able to understand and relate to Lois Jane when I couldn't, and often came to her defense when I discussed her sensitivity with him. She was spending more of her free time alone than I thought wise, but Jim encouraged me to be gentler with her. She never openly rebelled, but I could often tell how she was feeling by the way she walked or what she chose to wear to school. What I saw occasionally scared me, but Jim never lost confidence in her.

Jimmy had graduated from high school in early June and was offered athletic scholarships to two junior colleges. He accepted the wrestling scholarship at Bend. We wanted to do something special for Jimmy's graduation, but I was still weak from the infection. We finally settled on taking him to Hawaii. The party grew larger when we shared our plans with my parents. Daddy seldom wanted to travel, but he surprised us by agreeing to go when Mom insisted. It was a beautiful trip, even though I had to rest a lot.

We made other trips after school started that fall. Sometimes they were east to Bend to attend Jimmy's wrestling events. I took the bus over the mountains when the weather was bad.

I stayed in close touch with Patti. She and Frank moved back to Bellingham from Moses Lake and Frank became a project manager for Al. The growing company was now known as JIJ Construction. Patti went to work for a department store. She and Frank bought a home about the time Patti was promoted to buyer of women's clothing and she began producing fashion shows for local benefits. Their family seemed to be on a solid footing.

Things seemed to be going smoothly with all the kids and with Jim, and I felt better about myself than I had for some time.

During the period when I was drinking heavily, I had not attended church, but Lois Jane's godmother, Sandy Palmer, had picked Lois up and taken her each Sunday. Soon Lis Ann joined them. What wonderful friends these godparents were!

The church was Episcopal, the denomination Jim had grown up in, and Lois Jane became a member when she was ten. Shortly after my bout with infection, my newly discovered sobriety made me feel worthwhile enough to turn again to God, and Jim and I began attending with them. I was so grateful to return to a church fellowship and sense the presence of God. The Episcopal pastor was Father Joe Russell. This church community proved to be invaluable a few years later.

In 1974, when we began clearing underbrush on our hilltop property, I met my wonderful friend, Maggie. Jim and I were walking across her property to get to ours, and she stopped us. Cool and stern, weighing less than a hundred pounds, this tiny, wiry, old woman told us that we were to ask her permission each and every time we wanted to cross. No-nonsense and fearless, she intrigued me. After several months of politely knocking on her door to ask permission to cross her property, I was delighted when one day she invited me in for a cup of coffee.

Maggie was born in 1894 and had lived on the hill for most of the past fifty years. She shared many stories with me about her late husband, Ralph, and their life together. They had been very much in love.

She had lost a son and daughter at about the same time Ralph died and was still grieving when I met her, but her spirit was too strong for grief to overpower. Maggie made patchwork quilts, baked her own bread, grew beautiful flowers, and heated her house with an old wood stove. I often helped her bring wood from my property to store in her shed.

I began to visit her more frequently, and soon we were touching base by phone almost daily. If I needed to talk or just wanted a break, I'd call and say, "Maggie, I'm thinking of coming out for something to eat." Her answer was always, "I can't think of anything I'd rather have happen." When I arrived the coffee would be ready and my favorites, a slice of fresh-baked bread and cheddar cheese, would be waiting at my place at the kitchen table.

Maggie supported me through my struggles to balance my own emotional needs with the needs of my family and business. It wasn't long after our friendship developed that David became ill and I truly came to depend on her wisdom and love to get me through the hard times.

David was doing well at South Albany High School, excelling at everything. Jim and I were both proud of our son. He was big and his coach encouraged him to think seriously about playing college football. Since this meant putting on more weight, we shopped for special foods and he began lifting weights to build himself up.

All went well for a while, until he began having a recurring problem with his shoulder. It had once been dislocated, and would occasionally "go out" for no apparent reason. Surgery was recommended, and he entered the hospital to have the problem corrected in January 1975. His doctor called me the evening before the surgery was scheduled to tell me David's white blood cell count was extremely low. We went in the following morning to discover he had been moved to an isolation ward to protect him from infection. We were astonished to discover that David apparently had all the early symptoms of leukemia! The doctors told us that even a mild infection could kill him. I called the family. Fred flew in from Alaska, Patti from Bellingham, and Jimmy came from college.

David came home after about a week but had to remain isolated for some time. We kept everyone but the immediate family and the tutor away, trying to protect him from his unknown enemy. There was no treatment and no explanation for his illness. He didn't have cancer, yet all indications were that it was imminent.

Praying for him gave me a measure of peace, but David seemed as alone in his affliction as he had as he struggled for life in that incubator so many years before.

"Are you afraid?" I asked him one day, trying to share his pain.

"Yes," he replied, the tears streaming down his face.

I felt close to David that day, as close as I could be, and the guilt I felt from the previous years of selfishness and drinking assailed me. Most of this guilt came from not having encouraged David spiritually, and I was unsure that he felt close to God. I considered myself responsible for this, but I had no answers. Meanwhile, daily, I feared the infection or onset of the leukemia that would take him from us.

One doctor suggested steroids. They would alter his physical development with possible irreversible side effects, but David was clearly in a pre-leukemic state and needed something. I was frantic, and for awhile could only focus on my own feelings. It wasn't until I found Jim sobbing at his desk that I began to realize how deeply David's illness was affecting him as well. I took Jim in my arms and held him for a long time before we finally began to talk about our fears.

"Jim, there must be a doctor somewhere who knows what is causing this."

"Let's get the best in the field," he replied.

"Why don't we call Arne and see what he thinks?"

Arne Dahl, Jim's brother-in-law, was a physician in Bremerton, Washington. We had often gone to him for advice and we did so again now. He recommended a specialist in Portland, Dr. Kane, who suggested that we work on the diagnosis rather than the treatment.

"David doesn't have leukemia yet," Dr. Kane said, "and until he does, we aren't going to treat him for it."

That doctor was a godsend, for the treatments which had been prescribed for David by others might have left permanent damage. He was in and out of the hospital many times for infections during the next few months. He might complain of a toothache or a sore toe and within an hour each time, we'd be at the hospital and his life would be hanging in the balance.

We spent many anxious days in the oncology unit where we saw other young people dying. I knew that David saw this, too, and his fear added to my own.

Because the doctors had no explanation for David's condition, in desperation, they tried sometimes frightening and extreme procedures. On one occasion they theorized that David's white blood cells might be adhering to the walls of his veins and arteries and perhaps they could be shaken loose if David's heartrate was accelerated dramatically for a period of time.

They gave him a drug to accomplish this. I watched as David's body began to tremble and then shake. Eventually, he was shaking so violently that the bed rattled. A doctor stood by during the entire treatment. I was terrified that David's heart would just stop.

I paced the hall, peering in each time I passed David's door. I could hear the jarring of the bed as I approached and could hardly bear to look in. How I wished Jim were with me. He was home, sick in bed. I called frequently to keep him posted and prayed that the procedure would work.

It, like everything that had been tried before, didn't help. David still had practically no white count.

Between crises, we tried to carry on as normally as possible. David went back to school and resumed his part-time job with us. Dr. Kane advised us against David's playing football that fall. Any injury could result in his death. Jim and I felt that David needed to make the choice himself. We let him know that we were strongly against it, but football had been such an important part of David's life. His future dreams were of playing college football. His decision to play, anyway, was agony for us. After the first day of practice, however, David came home, and told me tearfully, "Mom, I won't be playing football." We wept together over this loss.

Sometimes, as I watched those around me struggling with their fear of losing David, I thought of what a miracle he was. He was my biggest boy, my quiet boy, and he was beautiful. After his rough start in life, I'd had him for seventeen years the doctors had told me I would never have. I tried to brace myself to let him go now. I told myself to be grateful for the miracle years we had shared instead of concentrating on my fear and pain.

Dr. Kane finally suggested we stop trying to diagnose David's problem. The tests and probing had taken its toll, wearing David down both physically and emotionally. Dr. Kane felt there was nothing else we should do as long as the relapses responded to antibiotics. By now, this approach was a relief to all of us.

David graduated in June, 1976, entered Willamette University that fall, and did well. Even though he has not had a critical time with his health since high school, his condition exists today and is still a mystery.

Jimmy, Jim, Izzy, David, and Fred, 1975, during the time David was threatened with leukemia.

Fritz and Neldia Muenscher with their children at Fritz's eighty-fifth birthday. Back row: Bunny Zuidmeer, Elinor Montgomery, Fred Muenscher, and Izzy Covalt.

Chapter 13

Patti knew I was worn out from anxiety over David's health and our usual business pressures. "Let's relax and take the girls over to Donna's new ranch," she suggested. Donna Gill had closed Indian Ford and sold the land, but shortly after, she started a new ranch at Rock Springs.

Going to the ranch turned out to be a good idea for many reasons. It allowed me to share special times with Patti, Lois, and Lissie, and we had the opportunity to introduce Patti's girls, Courtney and Heather, to riding. The break worked wonders for me. I felt rejuvenated and ready for a new challenge.

In response to Patti's interest in the garment business, I soon found myself a partner in "The Clothes Trunk" in Bellingham. It was especially fun to be working on a project with my daughter. We remodeled the building she found to our own tastes and made several buying trips together to San Francisco. The boutique was successful in some ways, but it turned out that making money wasn't one of them.

Lois worked in the boutique during that first summer and did very well. She was often top sales person of the week, a significant plus for her. I was pleased that Lois had another opportunity to excel, which she did in so many areas. Still, I was always aware of a dark side of her nature, a sensitive moodiness which worried me.

Unfortunately, my concerns were soon justified. Lois had gone out on a date and hadn't returned at the prescribed time. I worried and waited up for her as I always did when any of the kids were out. They had all been instructed to call if they would be late getting in, but Lois didn't call. When she and her date finally returned, I scolded her in front of him, knowing I was embarrassing her, but wanting to make my point. She quietly went to bed.

The next day was Mother's Day and Jim and I decided to take the girls to a restaurant. Lis Ann was ready on time, but I didn't get any response from Lois Jane's room on the intercom. Jim went to get her and returned quickly with Lois lying limp in his arms, and with a large, half empty aspirin bottle in his hand. We got her to the hospital where they pumped her stomach, but it was too late. The aspirin was already in her system and she went into convulsions.

Jim helped hold her down to keep her from being injured. He had recently been having unexplainable fatigue and shortness of breath, and even with my worry about Lois, I saw that the effort taxed him severely. I was afraid he would collapse trying to restrain her. Lois finally quieted, but the doctors warned us she might suffer heart failure. They moved her into the intensive care unit. I paced back and forth, terrified that she might not survive. I was also carefully watching out for Jim, who was white-faced and perspiring freely from his exertion.

Lois recovered, to our grateful relief, and we went immediately into family counseling. We also arranged private counseling for her. Father Joe helped a great deal, and over the next few months the lines of communication began to open.

I began now to worry about Jim's health. It didn't occur to me to worry about my own. It had now been two-and-a-half-years since my bout with the kidney infection and my last drink. Prior to that, my health had been astonishingly good and I seemed to get better and stronger as I stayed away from alcohol.

However, my menstrual periods had always been sparse and few since they began and they suddenly became abnormally heavy. I awoke one night lying in a pool of blood and awakened Jim. He got Jimmy to carry me to the car and they rushed me to the hospital where I went directly into surgery. Here I was again, fearing for my life. The surgeon stopped the hemorrhaging and I went home to the hospital bed in the living room again. My sister Elinor came for awhile to help. When I had regained sufficient strength, I went back into the hospital for a hysterectomy to remove fibroid tumors.

My recovery went well and I was grateful to be able to join the family gathering to celebrate Thanksgiving. The kids and Jim spent the morning in the kitchen preparing a special feast. All the children were home for the holiday. From my bed, I could hear and enjoy their fun and closeness.

It wasn't long before I was back on my feet again, and I felt better than ever, both physically and emotionally. Reconnected to God, and active in church, I had not felt this "together" since high school. Little did I know how much I would need this renewed strength in the months to come.

Both Salem restaurants were struggling. We tried various ideas to make them more profitable. But more alarming, Jim's health was worsening. His doctors couldn't figure out why. His shortness of breath and lack of energy often made it necessary to cancel business appointments. He had a complete physical that fall and discovered his kidneys were functioning at only twenty percent. We were told nothing could reverse the decline and he must get even worse before they would consider dialysis or a transplant. He would be at risk with either course of action. Plus, there would be the difficulty of finding a donor organ when the time came. In any event, dialysis would begin sooner or later, perhaps in one to five years, "when he got bad enough." I sobbed as Jim held me in his arms the night we got the news.

"We'll beat this thing, Iz." Always the optimist, Jim made me believe him.

He was ordered to get more rest. This prescription was, in some ways, a relief for both of us. We went into a survival mode: Jim fighting for his life and me taking care of the business. The only treatment for Jim was to adjust his diet and to rest without feeling guilty about it. I continued to discuss everything with him, and he participated as best he could with feedback and emotional support. But I now found the responsibilities of running the business without him, especially since things weren't going well, too great a burden. We were in the wrong mode, reacting to crisis instead of expanding and pushing ahead.

Son Fred, now twenty-five, had been a three percent stockholder in JIJ, Al's construction company, but had become disappointed and quit. I had encouraged him to start his own construction company in Alaska, but he wasn't happy doing that, either.

We talked when he came home in October 1976 to see Jim. We offered Fred one-third of the corporation to come in as a partner, and agreed to give him an option on half of the stock should either of us die. I think he needed us as much as we needed him and he agreed. He stayed on in Albany and stepped back into the business as though he had never left. I was glad to have my boy back home.

We began to retrench. Jim suggested that we sell North Salem. His sister, Margo, and her husband, Arne Dahl, were looking for career opportunities for their oldest boy Sande who had just returned from Vietnam. To our relief, they bought the restaurant, and Sande took over the management of it.

We had already sold one-third of Great Falls to our manager, Jack Drake, in the hope that he would hold the costs down. It didn't work, but brother Fred was doing well and when he offered to buy out our share, we agreed. It was a financial break for us and a huge relief.

By 1977, Shakey's Incorporated was running into serious problems nationwide. Sales and profits were declining and they were making a major effort to turn things around. One of their focuses was a restaurant restoration and upgrading program. Jim and I dipped into our personal funds, Fred added all his savings, and we began remodeling the Corvallis restaurant. We added new products and made personnel changes in the Albany office as well as in the field. Fred was eager, determined, and involved in every aspect of the effort.

Rod Tripp still owned our building in Albany. Our twenty-year lease was about to run out and we talked to Rod about remodeling the restaurant. It wasn't in either of our best interests, however, and we began building on a site we had acquired in South Albany.

We continued to be active members of the SFDA, as the

"Shakey's Franchise Dealers Association" was known. In 1976, I had been elected to the board of directors and in 1977, the board elected me secretary. As a result, I attended many nationwide board and committee meetings, which meant more responsibilities and more travel.

About this time, Shakey's Incorporated was purchased by the Hunt Brothers of Dallas, Texas. I met Lamar Hunt at the home of another franchisee in Seattle. Board members from all over the United States had flown in for a magnificent dinner that evening. Jim was too sick to go, but Fred went with me. Lamar impressed me as a kind, good man.

Because he knew Jim and I were the first Shakey's franchisees and were known to be very much a part of the early development and growth of the company, he was interested in talking to me both as a person and as a business associate. I made a point of introducing him to Fred, and he spoke with us at length about our specific operations. I felt that we were at the verge of another golden period for Shakey's. I was excited and hopeful, and became even more committed to helping pull the company out of the current slump.

Jim encouraged me, and while I was busy with SFDA, he stayed occupied in several ways. He spent most of his time being a father to Lois and Lis, and was supportive of Frank and Patti when they started their own construction business. With Lis Ann's help, he took both Courtney and Heather to Disneyland that summer. Despite his illness, Jim had decided that this was an important thing to do for his granddaughters, and to this day they remember their "Bapa" and their trip with him to Disneyland.

Even as he became sicker, Jim stayed involved with the Palmer family, to whom we were all very close. The oldest son, Steve, contracted cancer and was very ill. We all loved Steve, especially Fred, who had been Steve's close friend since third grade.

After an illness of a-year-and-a-half, Steve died in February of 1978 at age twenty-six. It was a blow to all of us and his illness distracted us from Jim's problems for awhile. Jim was still up and dressed for part of each day and spent much of his time out of bed with Steve and the Palmers. I talked to Steve for a few minutes the day before he died. We both knew this would be our last visit. He showed me the gold cross and chain he had bought for his mother as a goodbye gift, and we talked and said our own goodbye. He was such a sweet and loving boy and had shared so much of himself as his illness had progressed. He had been in such pain that it was a relief to know he would no longer have to suffer. I pulled myself away and left that day for an SFDA convention. It was good to know that Jim would be there for Fred and the Palmers and the rest of the family while I was gone. Deep inside, I knew that by going to the convention I was avoiding the most intense time for George, Sandy and their kids. I wouldn't have to feel the pain so fully as I would have had I been there.

On March 26th, we celebrated Daddy's eighty-fifth birthday at Fred and Esther's home in Ten Mile. Our entire family attended church together that morning, including Jim. We had a joyous day of sharing, food, visiting with friends, and photo taking. It was Jim's last trip to the farm.

In May, Jim and I went to Lake Tahoe with George and Sandy Palmer. It had been one of Steve's favorite spots. He had even gone there with his brother, Rob, Fred, and a group of friends late in his illness. Jim and I wanted to take George and Sandy there. It would be good for all of us. But Jim spent most of the time in bed, propped up with pillows to help his breathing. The four of us attended Glen Campbell's show one night, and the tears ran down my cheeks as he sang "Amazing Grace," his closing number. Somehow I knew Jim and I would never share an evening like that again.

Within twenty-four hours, fluids built up in Jim's body to the point that he could barely breathe. We took him to the Reno hospital, where they were able to give him relief. Always hopeful, he wanted to get home where he might get on dialysis. His kidneys were failing.

Chapter 14

I returned from Lake Tahoe with a feeling of misgiving. I think George and Sandy felt it, too. Jim and I simply couldn't bring ourselves to talk about the possibility of his death, and during the next couple of months, a new tension began to develop between us. I tried not to dwell on it, but the reality of his condition was on my mind constantly.

He appeared to age rapidly as his illness progressed. His tissues swelled to enormous size as they retained more and more water. I finally tried to talk with him about it, but his limitless optimism overwhelmed me. His answer was always, "I'll get on dialysis soon. It will be okay," or, "I'll get on the list for a transplant."

He never gave up believing he would somehow be cured.

Unable to discuss it openly, and unable to penetrate his wall of optimism, I sometimes found myself wanting to scream. The frustration built up to a point where I went to Father Joe for help. He seemed to understand our situation and visited us at home where he could talk to us, both individually and together. Father Joe told me to lean on Jim for emotional support. He felt Jim was still strong and that I needed to be honest with him about how I felt. He also suggested we begin expressing our concerns by writing short letters to each other about these feelings. I began my first letter by telling Jim how much I loved him, and went on:

> "We have talked about your illness in a very clinical way with much caution and reserve. Today was the first time we were both more open about our feelings. Right now I feel very close to you and almost as though everything will be all right, but now that I have one moment of that great feeling, I know things cannot ever be as they once were.
>
> "Now I feel emotional and sad that just wanting things to be right isn't going to make them that way."

I came down with the flu and wasn't feeling good when I received this from Jim:

"Hi, Iz. It's mid-afternoon and a quiet spot, so maybe it's time to mull a few thoughts. Did you think it was odd, your illness coming on so rapidly? It was as though you had permission to experiment in being dependent for a spell.

"Yesterday's crossing over must have been like a catharsis that let some of your defenses down, both physical and mental.

"I still feel I have a physical reserve that I haven't used yet. I do feel bad that this caused you so much concern. I hope sister Bunny can join you soon, as she will be a real lift to both of us."

I replied:

"I feel better now that I have talked to Dr. Froom to get some more guidelines. I know how you want to avoid that machine as long as possible, and I want you to, when I am rational. Somehow it seems at times (like today) that we are waiting for the bomb to drop and maybe if it dropped it wouldn't be so bad. It makes no sense at all, I guess. We just have to keep taking one step at a time. I love you and don't like seeing you so sick. Not feeling good I can live with."

Jim:

"I felt the job you did on the bank loan was a stroke of good work. Your tiff with Fred this morning seemed to have cleared the air and a lot of the problems that seemed to be insurmountable are clearing away. I feel better about our enterprise. I do worry about your health in that you will push too far and have a relapse. Please don't let it happen. I think my physical condition is not much changed by the flu. Please try not to worry too much and keep sharing with me. I am good for it."

Me:

"My spirits rose today to have you at the office for a while, and to see you dressed also made me feel much better. Strange how things affect a person. Somehow it made you seem healthier to me. I guess you can tell that my thoughts are on your health a good deal of the time, unless I am wrapped up in business, too much, I think, for good mental health."

Jim:

> "I am sitting in the chair watching young Jim preparing a gourmet dinner. He looks like he knows what he is doing. The off-and-on-again pressure such as illness, feeling better, then worse again. Loan unsureness: maybe, maybe not. First having a contractor, then not having a contractor. Gets really tough."

Me:

> *"I feel very down and am just glad to be withdrawing into the bedroom by myself. Seems to me you have been up and going quite a while yourself today. You must be tired."*

It was a relief when Jim was finally approved for dialysis. He traveled to Portland three days a week for treatment, hiring a driver to take him. He would leave the house about five each morning to return around five in the afternoon. He came back from these sessions completely exhausted and had to stay in bed most of the next day to recuperate.

Sometimes our friends Rod Tripp, George Palmer, or Frank Fisher would drive. This made the trip easier and more secure for Jim. I know their fellowship helped him a great deal through the long days of travel and treatment.

One evening Jim and I went out to a favorite Chinese restaurant together. I sipped tea and talked and talked. We were on familiar ground and it was wonderful to have him out of bed, dressed, and giving me his full attention. I was having such a good time I didn't notice the beads of sweat running down his face.

"Iz, I've had enough. We had better go home."

I looked closely at his face and felt awful when I realized how uncomfortable he was. It was our last evening out together. I felt Jim slipping away after that. I wanted him to talk to me about leaving, but in spite of our letter writing, neither of us ever did. He only talked about getting well. My reaction to this was a mixture of despair, sadness, and frustration. I was sure Jim's hope of getting well was only a fantasy.

I had momentary distractions. Even though Jim's health worsened and demanded so much of my emotional energy, I found myself getting involved in new business projects that would require me to focus my energies away from him. Perhaps this was my way of coping.

The SFDA board was one such distraction, but there were others. Our CPA and friend, Don Brudvig, called and asked me to join with other community leaders to organize a savings and loan association. I became the vice-president of what would one day become "Future Savings and Loan" and helped recruit other board members. We needed to sell more than a million dollars worth of stock to satisfy government regulations, and I invested fifty thousand of those dollars. We would open the bank in the summer of 1980.

Then there was the on-going debate with Shakey's Incorporated. We had been concerned about the renewal of our franchise agreement which would expire in 1979. Our franchise clearly stated that we could renew under the terms and conditions of the original contract we had developed with Shakey. We had applied for the renewal, expecting these conditions to be met by the corporation. We heard nothing for months. The Hunt Brothers were essentially trying to change the conditions of our franchise to favor the corporation.

Everything we owned was tied up in this business. We needed the security of having a new contract in hand. Shakey's lack of professional follow-through became an additional source of stress. I began to doubt their integrity.

These franchise concerns were pushed to the background of everybody's awareness by a sudden crisis in the family: Jim had a heart attack.

He had just finished dialysis when it happened. Fortunately, Jimmy and David had driven him to Portland that day and were present. It scared them, but Jim was grateful they were there. The hospital held him in intensive care for the next ten days.

The stress of dialysis was taking its toll, and though Jim longed for a transplant, I knew his chances were slim. The heart attack occurred in July. The earliest he could be considered for an appointment to begin the transplant process would be in February.

Then joy in the form of Bobbie Hutchinson came into our lives. Fred brought her home to meet us in early August. They said they were in love and planned to be married. Jim and I were sitting in the family room at the time. I remember how beautiful she was. She had long slender legs and was holding her cat. I knew their love was sincere and that things would work out for them.

They were married in September in Eugene and Jim managed to attend. Al and his new wife, Paulette were there, too. Al's marriage to my cousin, Erna, had ended in 1976. Jim and I had met Paulette before, and I liked her. She had been an airline stewardess whom Al had met on one of his trips to Fiji. We found a sitter for them so they could leave their new baby at our house during the wedding.

Since Fred knew Jim would need to rest as soon as possible after the ceremony, he arranged for the wedding reception to be held at our house so that everyone could be together. It was a great party. Over two hundred people came, including our family from Washington and Montana. Fred and Bobbie were off to a good start.

Also in September, Lois Jane enrolled in the Washington State College Veterinary School at Pullman and David enrolled in a business administration course in Las Vegas. He specialized in hotel and restaurant management. Jimmy continued his history major at the University of Oregon. Everyone was busy and occupied, but Lois was homesick by the end of October and called, wanting to come home to see her dad. I told her to stay in school and plan to come home for Thanksgiving. She reluctantly agreed.

Then, quite suddenly, George Palmer died. He had been running a high fever and was hospitalized a few days in Albany before being transported to St. Vincent's Hospital in Portland. The antibiotics had no effect on what turned out to be a blood infection. Jim was affected deeply by this loss. Despite his own grief, he shifted his concerns to George's family. He managed to help Sandy with legal forms and pension applications, and attended the funeral, although with great difficulty. Jim came home from the funeral exhausted, his reserves entirely depleted.

The following Monday morning, November 13, 1978, Jim left for Portland and dialysis, while I left for Kansas City and a long-scheduled SFDA Board meeting. The meeting was still in progress Tuesday evening when Gordon, the president of our association, was called to the phone. He returned to the room to let me know the phone call was actually for me. It was Fred. He was sobbing and could barely talk, but he managed to get out, "Dad died."

The fear of this moment had been haunting me for months, but the impact it had on me was totally unexpected. I went numb all over and fell to my knees with the phone in my hands. All I could think about was getting home to be with the kids, and I couldn't see through my tears. My rock, my biggest booster, my love, was really gone.

It would be years before I would be able to focus objectively on the loss I felt at that moment, to feel the reality and the pain of it, and to allow it to pass through me and not over or around. Knowing the risks hadn't helped. Nothing, not the letters we wrote to each other, nor conferences with doctors and family, had prepared any of us for the emptiness.

Later, I would find out the details of Jim's death. Jim had been at home recovering from his previous day's bout with the machine. Lis had found him when she returned from school that afternoon. At first she thought he was asleep, but she called Fred when she realized something had happened. The paramedics were called but it was too late for help. He died from an aneurysm which ruptured while he was sleeping. His was a painless and instant death, a blessing.

I somehow managed to make some calls before my SFDA friends got me on the first available flight out of Kansas City. It meant traveling indirectly via Seattle, but this allowed me to join Patti, Frank, and Lois for the rest of the trip. Fred, Jimmy, and Lissie were already home, and Jimmy would meet David at the airport that next morning when he flew in from Las Vegas.

When my plane finally arrived in Seattle, it was after midnight.

I connected with Frank and Patti and discovered that Lois hadn't arrived. Fred had called her with instructions to get a flight from Pullman to Seattle via Spokane where she would meet us. When her flight arrived without her I called the college. She was still there. The shock had been too much for her and she simply couldn't function. Then I remembered a young man from Albany who was also attending Washington State. We contacted him, and he went to Lois' room, took her to the airport and got her on the plane to Seattle to meet us. I was grateful for this support.

On the way home, I pondered how I could fill the hole Jim had occupied in the lives of the kids. I knew I could never take his place. We arrived in Albany about noon to an intensely sad but busy household. Friends kept calling and dropping in to offer their condolences. We were all exhausted but uplifted by the warmth and caring of all our friends and family. Father Joe was there and spent time with each of us individually. He was a great source of strength. He understood how helpless the children felt and gave each one an assignment, encouraging them to write something about their dad that could be shared with everyone. Later, at Jim's service, their writings were read aloud. This is what they wrote:

Patti:

> *"Dad—You told me to smile first if I wanted a smile, to say hello first if I wanted a greeting, and to love if I wanted love.*
>
> *"You expected a lot from us because you thought we were wonderful. If we were wonderful, that's why. You expected, but you didn't judge. We brought you problems and got direction, support and love.*
>
> *"Thank you for your love—it has made loving easier.*
>
> *"You are my example of the husband, the father, and the strength that I want to share with other families, with my children, with my husband.*
>
> *"My hope now is for all of your grandchildren to be raised with your strength, to know you through us, to learn about caring and loving the way we did."*

Fred wrote:

> *"How a man so different from myself could understand and love me so much is amazing. Being with you has been the most positive influence my life has seen. Thanks, Dad."*

Jimmy:

> *"Dad, you're only a memory to me now, and I can't believe it. I know I will hear that it was all a part of God's infinite design. This is no particular comfort. You were the*

foundation of my reality and it's been radically altered by your death. In my design, my fat babies would have been bouncing on your knee.

"I think the thing I'm going to miss most, although I'm not sure, are our conversations. Conversation with you was usually interlaced with, `Son, when I was your age, I was going through the same thing.' We finally established that raising children was a means of learning about yourself. We taught each other, Dad.

"Dad, whatever state or manner of existence you occupy, if any, I love you and was not ready for your death. We still had so much to teach each other."

(From the time he was a little boy, David always spoke with such caution and so softly that Jim had sometimes called him "The Whisper.")

David wrote:

"The Whisper has one final thing to say—
this time loud and clear, "I love you."
Thanks, Dad."

Lois Jane:

"Dad was many people's best friend, mine too. He felt a lot of my emotions, sharing thoughts, advice, and always much concern, with love. Dad loving me, made me love myself."

Lis Ann:

"My dad is strong and has the biggest heart you could find anywhere. My dad's heart is always bursting with love.

"He's always there when you need him and I know that everybody loves him. Why you ask? Because he's my dad. I love you."

We all gathered at the house after Jim's funeral. Many of the same people were there who had so recently attended Fred and Bobbie's wedding in September. I was grateful for their love and support. Jim's spirit had touched them all.

The days passed quickly after that, but the nights dragged on forever. I felt so alone when I went into the bedroom we had shared for so long, where Jim had been forced to spend so much of his last days. I had lain awake in that bed listening to Jim's labored breathing for months. Now it was too quiet.

I still find myself visualizing that last day when Lis Ann came home after school and didn't get a reply to her "Hi, Dad, I'm home." Jim and she loved each other so. It hurts me to think of her shock and pain when she walked in and discovered him.

Our good friend Rod Tripp called a few days after the funeral and asked how I felt about starting a scholarship fund in Albany's two high schools in memory of Big Jim Covalt. I discussed it with the family and everyone thought it a wonderful idea. Rod contacted other community leaders and before long the fund was established. It was large enough to award two annual scholarships at each school. I have a great satisfaction in knowing Jim's values and his name will continue to influence others, even though he only lived to be forty-eight years old.

Izzy with Jim and all six children at her brother Fred's home in Ten Mile, 1978, about six months before Jim's death. Back Row: Patti, David, Lis Ann, Jimmy, Lois Jane, and Fred.

Chapter 15

The days following Jim's death were full of agony for all of us. In a haze of anguish and grief we each did the best we could to survive. I don't remember much of what happened during those days. The finality of Jim's death surged through my body over and over. It was a deep physical ache that washed over me whenever I thought about him being gone. Then the picture of our three big boys at the funeral clinging to me and sobbing would pass in front of me. It was too much, and I stopped myself from thinking these thoughts.

I asked myself when I would ever feel good again—maybe never.

I was trying to block strong feelings of guilt and remorse. I could have chosen to be with Jim more, worked less and traveled less, driven him to Portland for dialysis more often myself rather than depending on a hired driver or a friend. The truth was that it was more comfortable for me to not watch his large frame blow up and distend with fluid retention, not to see the grey color of his face which beaded with sweat after any exertion.

Then came anger because I felt that he could have improved his health and maybe had another good ten years with us if he had not been so sedentary and if he had practiced better eating habits. This was followed with thoughts about all of the wonderful traits that he had and about how much all of us would miss his gentleness, patience, understanding and wisdom.

My decision to start drinking again wasn't a conscious one, but Bobbie and Fred invited me to spend Thanksgiving in Eugene with Bobbie's parents, and drinks were served that evening. The alcohol helped drown my feelings and thoughts. I was aware of what I was doing, but grateful for the relief. I decided that if I were careful, maybe I could have a drink now and then. Maybe alcohol really wasn't a problem for me. In the months that followed, I drank, but with moderation.

On December 10th, David's twenty-first birthday, I flew to Las Vegas where he was attending college. It seemed important that I be with him. I stayed one day and came home.

On December 16th, we opened our bright new restaurant

building in Albany. It had been under construction at the time of Jim's death. The transition from the old building went smoothly and business was better in the new location than it had been in the old one. Worry about regular customers being unable to find us had been needless.

The family decided to meet at Patti and Frank's home in Bellingham for Christmas that year. Our traditional family Christmas could never be the same without Jim. Santa came to delight Courtney and Heather, but it wasn't the Santa we all remembered. Our time together was filled with pain.

Those who could get away spent the week between Christmas and New Year's Day with me in Albany. I worked part of the time. Being together helped us all get through the holidays. Lois Jane was reluctant to return to school when the time came. I tried to encourage her, reminding her of what her dad would have wanted, but she kept to herself and I grew even more concerned. She seemed quiet and withdrawn.

I was relieved when she left for school, thinking she was back on track and would be okay. But it was a short respite. An emergency call came from the Dean of Students a few days later. Lois had attempted suicide again. I was stunned. As before, she had taken an overdose of aspirin and was in a coma. I sat propped with pillows all that night, afraid the phone would ring again and bring news I couldn't bear to hear. I wanted to go to her but I had been instructed to wait. She was being flown to Spokane and was in imminent danger of kidney or heart failure. The second phone call came and this time it was her doctor. Lois was now in intensive care and still critical. He advised me to wait some more. I called every hour until the critical time was over. Finally I could go to be with my sweet baby girl.

The memory of her wanting so much to come home in October to see her dad haunted me now. She had desperately missed him when she went away to school. My own rigidity and fears for her success had not allowed for that kind of behavior. Now Lois Jane needed her dad and I needed him to help me. Jim would have given me wisdom and strength. All I could come up with for an answer was "we need to work harder."

Patti and David flew to Spokane with me to be with Lois when she came out of intensive care. We found her spiritless, drained both emotionally and physically. Counseling and medication helped when she returned home, but she gave up on school and went to Bend to work for Donna Gill at the ranch.

I attempted to leave my concerns behind when I accepted an invitation from Ardelle Marchand to go to Hawaii with her. As it rained nearly all the time we were there, the highlight of my day became my after dinner benedictine and brandies. During the day I ate M & M's, napped, and counted the days until I could leave.

When I returned, I threw my energy into the Future Savings and

Loan enterprise. I attended board meetings and actively sold stock in the bank. The organizational and planning meetings were held in our conference room at Covalt Enterprises. We needed to sell one million dollars worth of stock in order to open, and I was responsible for selling at least a tenth of it. Most of my sales were small, ranging from one to three thousand dollars. This required a lot of effort, but I believed in the idea. I think those who bought shares from me did so because they believed in me.

Then there were other concerns. The dream house Jim and I had designed was still under construction on the twenty-acre wooded hill I had purchased so many years ago. We had been excited about it, but now I could no longer generate any enthusiasm for the house. All the details, including a dialysis room, had been designed with Jim in mind. While I felt compelled to finish the project, there was no joy in it.

My competent and loving daughter Patti stepped in to offer encouragement and help with decisions. She spent hours looking at colors and scanning endless lists, pulling me in as she could. I left everything else up to the contractor. I might have visited the site more frequently had my friend, Maggie, been home. We had looked forward to being neighbors, but her family had moved her to a nursing home when her mind began to fail. The hill was lonely without her.

Patti helped me move into the new house when it was finished, but suggested I continue to live part of the time in the house in town until I felt better. She thought I needed time to get used to the new place without Jim, and she was right. I divided my time between the new house and the town house for about a year.

In addition to helping me with the house, Patti still had the Clothes Trunk. She was relieved when I suggested we give it up. The continued financial losses had placed her under a great deal of stress and she was justifiably discouraged. We decided to take our losses and I helped with a close-out sale in February, 1979.

We also had major changes in our restaurant business to consider. The agreement Jim and I had made with Fred when he came in with us gave him fifty percent of Covalt Enterprises when Jim died. We set about reorganizing the company.

Jim and I had done well with our restaurants for quite a few years, but made the mistake of not reinvesting enough in new ideas, decor, and updated products. Customers need change and a fresh approach. Employees need continuous training. We had failed to provide either of these. Nor had we built a strong enough cash reserve to respond to these needs. It is easy to look back and view the mistakes.

Fred and I knew we needed to modernize South Salem as we had Corvallis. We either had to borrow in order to upgrade and trust the effort would pay off, or close it. We decided on the latter, but needed an alternative plan, since the building was leased and we were responsible for the rent for several more years. This complication prompted a partnership between Fred, me, and three of his friends to turn it into a tavern. One of the partners managed it and the project was successful.

At the same time, the lease on our old Pizza Pantry near the University in Corvallis was coming up for renewal. The restaurant was no longer profitable. Revitalizing was necessary to improve its potential. We felt the addition of a beer license might do it. Our application caused an official reaction from the University, which opposed an alcohol license so close to the campus. The city denied our application. The Pizza Pantry had been an integral part of our early growth and I hated to close it, but reality dictated otherwise.

These decisions left us with two successful restaurants, Albany and Corvallis, and we were again on a sound financial footing, benefitting from our updated facilities and our new products, specifically the salad bar.

It felt like time to consider a third restaurant. The first Shakey's in Eugene had closed years earlier, so we reclaimed that city as part of our franchise area. Fred and I began negotiation with Fred Meyer's executives to build a restaurant for us in Eugene. While this might have been an exciting and fun challenge for me, it wasn't. I instinctively knew how to put together what we refer to as a "package" for starting a new restaurant and I simply went through the motions without any heart or feeling. Fortunately, Fred had enough enthusiasm and energy for both of us, and the construction went smoothly.

When the Hunt Brothers bought the Shakey's chain, they replaced many key management people. Some of them lacked the necessary experience for their position. The effect of this was that Shakey's reduced services while increasing demands on their franchisees. This hurt some people even more than it hurt us, but the unsettled state of the corporate office was hurting us, too.

The continuing problem with the renewal of our franchise with Shakey's added a great deal of anxiety to my life. June 19th was the twentieth anniversary of our Albany opening and the due date for the renewal of the franchise. I had been trying to obtain the renewal for months, and as the expiration date approached, I was in an almost constant state of stress and my bouts with hyperventilation returned. Our franchise agreement called for Shakey's to renew, at our option, under the same conditions as the original, but each new contract they sent contained added restraints, higher royalties, and increased controls.

I wrote or called them frequently with my concerns as the deadline approached, but couldn't seem to get my point across. Discouraged and disillusioned, I wrote a final letter notifying them that I would need to have the correct contract available for my signature by mid-March or I would proceed with plans to do business under a different name. When Shakey's didn't respond, we got serious about striking out on our own.

"On our own" was a thought which left me both excited and chilled at the same time. One of the advantages to having a franchise is the benefit of using an established, widely advertised, well-known name. But more importantly, I was afraid of the wrath we might suffer from the powerful Hunt Brothers. I had cause to worry, but we had no recourse but to proceed with our new plans.

What name would we use if not "Shakey's?" What would have the right sound to catch the imagination of the public? We would have to build our image from scratch. After much family debate we finally arrived at "Izzy's Pizza Restaurant." Daughter Patti designed the logo. We ordered new signs, rewrote and printed new menus, made changes in our pizza and sauce recipes, and redecorated each restaurant just enough to establish a new identity within our budget. City, county, state, and federal offices all had to be notified, licenses changed, and new forms ordered.

These moves finally got Shakey's attention. I began receiving calls and visits by executives from all levels of the corporation. In May, the president of Shakey's, Don Smith, arrived in Albany. I refused to see him. Fred, however, met with him and explained how we had tried for eighteen months to renew our franchise and had been ignored. The president offered concessions, but we had invested so much time and money in the change that it was too late for us to turn back. More importantly, our trust was gone. They had said they were ready to talk many times before. Why should we believe they would follow through this time? And, there was principle to stand on.

David, meantime, had transferred his credits from Las Vegas and moved to Willamette University in Salem to be closer to home. He was having trouble concentrating in class and finally came to me one day with a plan to drop out. He wanted to go back to work at the restaurant. This scared me. I wasn't over the shock of Lois's suicide attempt and I felt my control over the family slipping further. I was also afraid for his future. I was afraid for all of us and I responded with:

"Well, David, go ahead, drop out, but I'm not going to. I'm going to keep going, and..."

I stopped suddenly, realizing what I was saying. I looked up to see tears running down David's face and a very different fear swept over me. What was I doing to my boy?

"Oh, sweetheart, you really are troubled, aren't you?"

"Yeh, Mom."

"Would you like to talk to Father Joe?"

"Yes," he managed to say. I called the church and Father Joe said for him to come in immediately.

David returned looking peaceful and much brighter. "I'm going to leave school, Mom."

"You are?" I was shocked by the outcome of his consultation.

"Yes. I need to work." And he did. He later enrolled in The Hotel

Restaurant Management program at Oregon State University and received his degree in 1982.

Jimmy graduated from Oregon State in June of 1979. He put himself through school by working and supplying his own funds. I was so proud of him.

He had done well and was considering post-graduate work in history, when my brother, Fred, contacted him. Fred owned fifteen restaurants at the time and was temporarily short a manager. Jimmy had worked in our restaurants, but had earned most of his college money as a laborer in the construction industry. He had no management experience. I had some misgivings about the opportunity, but Jimmy went ahead with it, and moved to Washington right after graduation. Not long after, on June 19, 1979, our "Shakey's" signs came down and "Izzy's" went up. Our customers never blinked. The name change had no measurable effect on sales.

In July, I received a shock. Bunny called to tell me that my dear baby sister, Elinor was very ill and was going in for surgery the next morning. I left for Bellingham, frightened and eager to get there. The doctors found cancer, and the prognosis was grim. We were devastated, especially Mom and Daddy. Bunny and I left after a couple days, shaken but grateful for Lonnie and for how close he and Elinor were.

Elinor proceeded with the difficult chemotherapy and we spent many months fearful of a relapse. During the crisis, Lonnie and Elinor continued to be supportive and loving of one another and their two teenage daughters, Mary and Annie. The family all kept in contact to get frequent reports on Elinor's progress.

Back home, Fred and I continued to fine-tune the new "Izzy's" image. The Fred Meyer chain went ahead with their plans to build our facility in Eugene under an "Izzy's" sign. We opened adjacent to their Santa Clara store in December 1979. In the thirteen months since Jim's death, Fred and I had closed two restaurants, turning one into a tavern, had established the "Izzy's" chain, and had already opened a third restaurant under the new name. Jim would have been proud of us.

All this time I had been very careful with alcohol. With a few exceptions, when I had B & B's after dinner with friends, I established rules for my drinking which would guarantee that I would drink with success. At first, I limited myself to one glass of wine after dinner. Gradually I increased this to two. Then I found I could have a glass before dinner and two after. I felt that I was in control. After awhile, I added a glass with dinner, too.

Eventually, my fear of alcohol relaxed and I stopped monitoring it so carefully. One evening I learned that my new relaxed attitude could lead to humiliation. It was to have been a special dinner at one of Albany's finest restaurants. The kids were there, along with several family friends, and drinks had been served. I'll never forget that night. It was November 14, 1979, the first anniversary of Jim's death.

At first I had simply relaxed and let my bourbon and water do its work. I was not interested in the food. I managed to make repeated trips to the bathroom to relieve my bladder. The next thing I knew I couldn't walk without help. Jimmy was assisting me back and forth. I felt the dampness of my skirt and even in my drunkenness I was appalled when I glanced down at my chair and saw the wet ring of urine on it. Jimmy finally talked me into an early departure. He and our good friend, Ed, soon got me into the car and delivered me home and to my bed. This was the first such episode since 1973, but it would not be the last.

This experience was just the beginning of a downward spiral to what I call "my bottom." I established new rules after this incident, which I followed carefully for the next year. But the new rules allowed me much more latitude than the old ones had. I could drink more kinds of alcohol more often. I told myself that I was in control. In reality, I was obsessed.

I was using alcohol and tranquilizers to suppress my grief and anxiety. Tranquilizers got me going in the morning. They quieted the withdrawal symptoms—inner shaking, fogginess, and queasy stomach, with which I awoke each day. During the day, they kept my emotions under control and kept me physically calm. In the evenings I could relax and have my "quota" of alcohol. This started the cycle again; drinking, withdrawal symptoms, and tranquilizers. It kept me from feeling too much.

Not only was I unable to deal with my own grief, I couldn't deal with seeing my children's pain. Nor could I see that my pulling away from them was adding to it. I didn't encourage them to talk to me about their feelings. Instead, I expected them to stay busy and productive, as I was, either in school or work.

Lis suffered quietly during this period, but she also showed support and concern beyond her years for me. I didn't see that she was concealing her fears, anger and grief. She had been used to spending time with her dad and missed him. She was carrying a huge burden alone and it would take years before these powerful emotions finally worked their way to the surface.

Although Patti and Frank were very busy too, as they had started construction of their new home in the summer of 1979, Patti visited many times and called me frequently. Unlike the others, the grief she was feeling was visible. She missed talking things over with Jim. More than once she said to me tearfully; "If only I could talk to Dad, I know he would understand." As close as Patti and I were, I was too practical for her at times. She could count on Jim to not only listen to her dreams, but to add to them.

When Jimmy's job with brother Fred ended, he came back to us, took additional training in our new "Izzy's" organization, and stepped in as assistant manager of our Eugene restaurant when it opened in December of 1979. Lois stayed with Jimmy in Eugene for awhile. He persuaded her to enroll in some classes at the University of Oregon, but she continued to be restless and without focus. It was 1980 by this time, and I saw little of Lois or any of the others as my drinking increased.

Chapter 16

Six months after the Shakey's signs came down, I heard from the Hunt Brothers, and it was terrifying. I was at home alone when I heard a knock on the door. I opened it to find a representative from the sheriff's department there to serve me papers naming us defendants in a potentially complicated and costly civil suit.

I had lived in fear of this for some time. We had been the first Shakey's franchisee and were well known to the other franchisees. The Hunt Brothers were obviously attempting to make an example of me. My brother Fred, sister Bunny, and a number of close friends were among Shakey's franchisees. I knew Shakey's was afraid my success in leaving the chain would cause others to do the same.

I was frozen with terror. I had visions of losing everything I owned. If Izzy's went down, I would be unable to help any of the kids financially in the future if they needed it. Jim and I had worked too hard and too long to see it lost in insurmountable debt. I immediately contacted Garry McMurray in Portland. Garry was the attorney who handled the successful class action suit the franchisee association had brought against Shakey's in 1971. Given Garry's assurances that we had a good case, we went into this legal fray with some hope, but with tremendous apprehension.

Preparation for the suit was expensive. The legal fees mounted daily, but we approached the trial with determination. We had no choice but to defend ourselves and now it consumed us. The jury trial began in Portland in mid-July and was over in fifteen days. All the kids attended part of the time and Fred was there every day. I felt we were literally fighting for our lives and I think the kids did, too.

I look back and realize how fragile I was during the trial. Patti discussed it years later and reminded me how I had a bar set up in my room so I could drink every night. I didn't know it then, but I drank to ease my tortured feelings. I carefully measured and monitored the prescription tranquilizers every day to help ease my discomfort. I managed to be up on time every morning, walk to the court house, and spend all day waiting to testify. When I was called I looked directly at the person I was speaking to and concentrated on keeping my emotions under control. And I did, except for one time.

I had been listening to one of Shakey's employees give his testimony and detected discrepancies in his story. I had known this individual for some time and suddenly felt betrayed. I cried out uncontrollably and collapsed under the strain. Two of my sons assisted me from the room.

Garry, justifiably, was upset at my display of emotion. He was afraid the judge would call a mistrial and we'd all have to go through it again, but the trial continued without interruption the next day. Then it went to the jury. We waited for hours at a nearby café while they deliberated. We won, but I was so drained by the experience that I had difficulty comprehending our triumph. What we had won was the right to go on with our lives.

We gathered at the house on the hill that night for a victory celebration, but I didn't feel the way I expected I would. Nor did I react as others probably thought I should. I didn't feel elated, I just felt dead. We had won, but I couldn't relax. It was over, but I couldn't sleep.

When news of the verdict spread, our phone rang constantly as friends, newspaper reporters, and people I didn't even know wanted to talk to me. Garry was afraid the additional publicity would prompt the Hunt Brothers to appeal, and suggested I not talk to them. It was easy to not talk. I didn't even have the energy or desire to share the victory with family or friends. I drank to try to relax and forget everything. But the alcohol didn't work and I didn't know why. I would sleep, have a bad dream, and awake in panic. To calm myself, I would get up and fix a drink to bring back to bed. This cycle repeated itself all night, every night.

Finally, after a few days, I called Ardelle Marchand. She worked for a doctor I knew in Everett, Washington, and I wanted him to hospitalize me, away from Albany. I simply wanted to sleep and I didn't want anyone to know what I was doing. Ardelle met my flight in Seattle and I was admitted to the Everett hospital. They put me to sleep and fed me intravenously for three days, waking me only long enough to use a bedpan. It was a great relief to finally sleep. Doctor Pete gave me strict orders as I left the hospital. I wasn't to drink, as the medication he prescribed wasn't compatible with alcohol. I agreed to this.

By this time Ardelle had told the kids what was happening. She took a week of her vacation to take me to a friend's cabin on Camano Island in the Puget Sound while I recovered. It was a beautiful spot and we walked on the beach together. She gradually reduced my medication and I went home, grateful for her help and friendship.

I intended to move back into my business responsibilities as I felt ready. I tried, but alcohol got in the way. Doctor Pete had put me in touch with a doctor in Corvallis to monitor my condition, who said I could have a few drinks during the holidays. I interpreted this to mean I could drink.

I wanted to relax, be with people, and have a good time. A festive New Year's Eve party would be just the thing. I called a friend and we attended a party in Portland, where I met an unusual man who appeared to have an unlimited capacity for alcohol. He didn't seem to mind my uncontrolled drinking, and we drank together all night. This lack of any constraints made him comfortable to be with and we became good friends. I managed to get home and continued to binge two more days. Then, to my astonishment, Bunny and Pete showed up on my doorstep. They told me that they had called the night before to tell me they would be by that morning. I had no memory of their phone call. I had blacked out. This was not the first time. Again, while in a blackout, I had functioned; talking, walking, eating and drinking. But my brain retained nothing.

It didn't occur to me that Bunny and Pete might notice anything strange in my appearance or behavior, and since I didn't want to alarm them by drinking so early in the morning, I began the day without any relief from my dull headache, queasy stomach, and an inner shaking feeling. It was distasteful to me to hear anybody talk about a hangover, and I certainly did not think of the suffering I was going through as such.

Then, in the middle of my grueling visit with Pete and Bunny, Fred called to tell me Bobbie was in labor and asked if I would come to the hospital to be with them. With all the drinking I had been doing for the last few days, I had forgotten that the baby, their first, was due. I wanted desperately to be there, yet it seemed to be a further imposition on me. Why couldn't the baby have waited a day or two? I was miserable, but I went.

Withdrawal symptoms began to torture me as the day dragged on. A drink would have relieved me, but Bunny and Pete were still there. Besides, I was at the hospital. I know now the only way I got through that day without a drink was by taking tranquilizers I had hoarded from a prior prescription.

The interminable waiting was horrible. Little Dean was finally born by Caesarean that evening and I remember how happy we all were, but I don't remember much else. It was a huge relief to get home where the late hour gave me an excuse to serve drinks.

My new "friend" of unlimited capacity began visiting me regularly a few days later. Because of convictions for drunk driving, he didn't have a driver's license. I would therefore pick him up at the bus station, and we would return to my house to drink.

It was then that I stopped visiting my friend Maggie. Because of her increasing senility she no longer recognized me, and I used that to ease my conscience. It was hard for me to see her in her current state, knowing that if she was aware, and could recognize that I was drinking, it would have hurt her deeply. My guilt kept me away.

Drinking relieved my misery, but I was making someone else's life miserable: my seventeen-year-old, Lis Ann, who was still in high school. Lis Ann knew what I was doing and tried to interfere with my drinking as much as she could. She later told me I would sometimes call out in the middle of the night for her to bring me a drink. She would usually comply, but would water it down in an attempt to curb my drunkenness. She often tried to ignore my requests, hoping I would fall back to sleep.

Such treatment during her all-important senior year must have hurt her, yet I perceived her reluctant attitude as rebellion. I gave her five hundred dollars soon after her eighteenth birthday in March, and told her to move out. I justified my action to the family by accusing her of not living by my rules. She moved in with strangers. I lost track of her for six weeks as she went from place to place, but I was more concerned with drinking than with anyone or anything else.

The next step in my downward spiral was to start drinking earlier in the day. My "friend" encouraged this, often handing me a drink to help me get over a hangover. I marveled at, and liked, his attitude towards drinking in the morning.

My work suffered, of course. I no longer had any desire to be at the office and had no interest in managing Izzy's. I would show up late, shuffle papers, and sign documents without thoroughly studying them. I wasn't even reliable about keeping appointments. My lack of focus and unreliability caused problems, but I was oblivious to all of them. Fred had to handle everything.

Then I had a success which reinforced my illusion that I was still under control. I managed to go an entire weekend without any alcohol! Bunny held a surprise party for Pete's sixtieth birthday in Missoula, and most of the family flew in for the event. I came prepared not to drink. Though it was difficult, I managed, using extra tranquilizers to replace alcohol for that weekend. It was such a relief to get home to my drinking.

I wasn't so successful a few weeks later when I took granddaughters Courtney and Heather on a train trip to Calgary. When Patti asked the girls about the trip, she became concerned when they mentioned how "Gaga" had acted after she drank. It was embarrassing to have Patti question me about it.

I remember my worst fear at this time was the family would think I couldn't control my drinking. Patti and the boys began to hint that they were worried. I told them I could handle it, that I had always been able to handle alcohol, and then quietly began reducing contact with them.

My second greatest fear was to black out and do something I wouldn't remember later. I began experimenting and discovered I could maintain a steady intake of a certain white wine without suffering blackouts. As long as I paced myself. The trick was to limit my intake to a half-gallon bottle per day.

Before long, however, I found myself buying two bottles a day and waking up in the morning to find I had opened the second one. When

I couldn't remember opening it, I knew I had blacked out again. I would worry for the rest of the day about phone calls or appointments I might have made while in a drunken stupor. If no one confronted me during the day about forgetting something, I would feel relieved, but the cycle would start all over again that evening. The stress this produced simply motivated me to drink more.

By now I started most days with heavy feelings of dread and anxiety combined with paranoia.

April 25th, we opened a new Izzy's in Bend, Oregon. I managed to attend. I drank wine and didn't eat. As the evening progressed, my speech became slower and more slurred. I continued to drink, and was weaving when I got up for my frequent trips to the restroom. Some friends unexpectedly invited me to their motel about halfway through the celebration. I later found they had done this to get me out of the restaurant. My obvious drunkenness had embarrassed Fred and the staff and I hadn't even been aware of it.

I felt miserable the next day and tried to drive back to Albany without drinking, but the hangover got worse until I reached the town of Sisters where I stopped and had a few drinks to ease my misery. I knew Patti was about to have her third baby and I wanted to call her, but didn't want my voice to sound slurred over the phone. I decided I couldn't drive any further and checked into a motel after picking up my customary two half-gallons of wine. My "system" of controlled intake worked this time, and I felt well enough to call Patti the following morning. She had given birth to Ashley the day before. I went to Bellingham to be with them. I thought I managed to stay in control, drinking only moderately, but Patti later told me I had repeatedly raided their liquor cabinet after the family had gone to bed.

I don't remember anything about Mother's Day that year. I know I didn't contact Mom, and I certainly didn't want anyone to contact me. My life now revolved around alcohol and I didn't want anything or anyone interfering with it.

Bunny called me shortly after Mother's Day and told me that she and Fred were coming for a visit. I couldn't figure out why they were coming, but I knew they would be in the way of my drinking. Little did I know, that was what was bringing them. The boys and Patti had called and asked them to come. My not drinking at Pete's birthday party had made Bunny and brother Fred think I was still in control, but Patti and the boys had finally convinced them I was in trouble. They planned to confront me together.

As it turned out, the boys decided that they shouldn't wait for them to arrive. This was Friday, May 15, 1981. I was puttering about the office, waiting for time to pass so that I could go home to my alcohol, when Fred asked me to come into his office. I was surprised to find Jim and David waiting there for me as well.

"Mom," Fred began, "we're worried about the amount of drinking you are doing."

I was stunned and responded with my usual denials, but Jim and David reminded me of how often they had seen me drink and of my obvious increase in consumption. I felt humiliated, fearful, and angry at the same time, and responded by telling them that they should all mind their own business.

"I can take care of myself and can stop drinking any time I want. I've done it before and I can do it again."

"We're worried about you, Mom."

"Okay, I'll show you. I'll stop today...right now."

The boys seemed relieved when I told them I would stop, but Jim followed me to the door as I was leaving. "Mom, we understand not everyone can stop by themselves. We checked into it, and there is help available if you need it." I heard what he said, but walked out of the office that day determined never to drink again!

The first thing I did when I got home was call my drinking "friend" in Portland to tell him I was quitting. I didn't know if I had convinced him. I didn't really care whether I had or not, but I wanted him to leave me alone. I didn't take another drink that day or the next two days, but the symptoms of withdrawal set in and I was lonely. I wanted to call someone, but couldn't think of anyone with whom I could share my growing sense of desperation. I couldn't sleep that weekend and was crazy with the need for relief. By Monday I began to think I was going to die.

I had seen a man die while going through DTs when I was in nurse's training. This horrid memory of delirium tremors was frightening and I began to wonder if it was going to happen to me. I could, I thought, take a drink and end the withdrawal.

I recognized for the first time that I truly was an alcoholic.

I would never drink for pleasure again, but I might have to drink for the rest of my life in order to stay alive. Despairing of ever having a life free of alcohol, I deliberately poured myself a drink, just enough to control the withdrawal symptoms. I would have to tell my family that alcohol was necessary for my very existence, hoping for their support and understanding.

I drank slowly, measuring each drink and pacing myself. I knew how much it would take from past experience to bring relief, but it wasn't long before I realized something was wrong. I wasn't getting my usual calm. Desperate now, I continued, measuring each drink and recording it to be sure. Carefully, in addition to the alcohol, I took Valium. My supply was running low, and I knew it would take a visit to the doctor to get a refill. Since I was in no shape to get to the doctor by this time, I worried about running out. The estimated quota of alcohol passed with little more than a slight reduction in chills and shaking. What was wrong?

I continued to sweat, was nauseated, and periodically passed out, but only for short spans of time. I desperately needed and wanted the relief of passing out. By Tuesday morning I was terrified!

Chapter 17

And now I was feeling a horrible lonely and frightening desperation. I feared that I would die without alcohol, but the alcohol was not bringing relief. Nothing helped. I couldn't drink and I couldn't not drink. I knew I would not be able to tolerate it much longer.

Then I remembered Jim's parting comment on Friday afternoon. "Mom, we understand not everyone can stop by themselves. We checked into it, and there is help available if you need it."

I called him on that terrifying Tuesday morning and said, "I need help, Son."

"I'll get right back to you, Mom."

Only a few minutes went by before Jim called back. "Can you hold on until Thursday, Mom?"

"I don't know."

"We can get you into Serenity Lane, a place where they treat alcoholism, on Thursday. It's in Eugene."

"All right...yes. I think so."

"We'll pick you up Thursday morning at eleven."

It was a long forty-eight hours. No one called, but the torture faded slightly. I think knowing the kids were there for me, that they would help, rekindled what faith I had. Also, the alcohol finally began to work enough to make life tolerable again. I continued my program of controlled drinking.

Fred and Jim arrived exactly at eleven. I was afraid to go without something to sustain me and walked out of the house with a six-pack of beer.

"Gee, Mom," Jim said, as I got in the car, "I would think you might want to make a better impression."

"Well," Fred injected before I could answer, "if I thought this was my last chance to drink, I might want to do it right up to the end, too."

As we drove away, I suddenly remembered this was the day Bunny was to arrive. Alarmed, I told the boys that someone needed to call her and Uncle Fred. I was shocked to learn that Bunny's visit was part of a plan to intervene with my drinking and that she was coming anyway to support me through the first days of treatment. It was such a comfort to know she would be there. What a dramatic shift in my attitude. Just a few days earlier I had dreaded her visit. Now I needed her.

An hour later I stood at the foot of the steps in front of Serenity Lane. I had reluctantly left what remained of the six-pack of beer on the seat of the car. Clutching my purse, which still had the remainder of my tranquilizers in it, I cautiously climbed the flight of stairs that led to the front door. I had no urge to turn back, because I felt a great deal of hope for what was inside. I finally reached the door, but it was locked. I realized later that we were locked in as well as out.

Someone came immediately when I rang the bell and showed me into an office where I was introduced to Shirley.

She would be my group counselor and would be with me for the entire stay. We later became friends. She interviewed me that first day and asked me questions about my health and experience with alcohol.

I was assigned to the "detox" room, but afraid to be alone, I found a bench near the nurses' station. Discomfort gradually gave way to nausea and uncontrolled trembling, followed by sweating and chills. Everything became blurred. Bunny arrived and I was gratefully aware of her presence. The hours passed slowly. I was in agony.

I had thought this would be a replay of my hospital stay in Everett. I wanted to be in bed and medicated. I thought all the patients would be. This wasn't what I had expected, and I didn't like it.

I couldn't feel emotion, or think. I had to focus on just surviving each moment. I was getting minimal doses of librium, but it had little effect. I was desperate for any relief.

The next morning I was given magnesium to minimize the possibility of convulsions. They also continued the librium to ease the withdrawal symptoms. The daylight made me feel I could make it a little longer. Bunny stayed three more days, until I left detox. Knowing she would come each morning helped me get through those first difficult nights when the shaking and shivering became unbearable.

On Sunday, I was assigned to a room and given a roommate. The end of detox meant the beginning of a strict daily regimen. I was astounded by the routine and what seemed to me to be unrealistic and harsh expectations. I also knew that my librium was being decreased daily, and that soon I would be getting nothing. It scared me. The inner shaking was still there and I craved more relief, but instead got less.

I was so frightened that I stopped Dr. Kerns in the hallway one day and told him how afraid I was of what was happening to my body.

"You don't need to be scared," he said. "We're watching you closely. When you needed to be afraid was before you got here."

This gave me more confidence and I participated more willingly in our morning exercises at the YWCA. Still, it always seemed like such a long walk back to the center.

After exercise each morning, we went to our assigned group meeting, where we worked for hours, sharing our lives and supporting each other. There were ten of us in Shirley's group. I was pleased that I had been assigned to Shirley because I had felt some connection when she had interviewed me the first day. About a third of my group were women. This same two-to-one ratio of men to women prevailed throughout the treatment center. I noticed that non-smokers were rare. Of the constant population of thirty patients, only one or two didn't smoke.

At my first group meeting I introduced myself. "My name is Izzy and I'm an alcoholic."

Introducing myself as an alcoholic seemed strange. I forced myself to go through the motions, because I knew that was expected of me. This was the first of many things I did by rote, simply because they told me I must.

One of our first assignments in group was to write a detailed history of our life with alcohol. We were to begin with our early memories and attitudes toward it, and continue with all the details that led to Serenity Lane. This was an especially difficult assignment for me for many reasons. The first, of course, is that it was highly emotional. Also, I felt physically unable to cope with this stressful introspection. I was still shaking all the time. I had to concentrate to hold the pencil, and just getting my feelings on paper was a slow and tedious process. Plus, I had difficulty getting my eyes to focus.

The assignment was to be done in our free time, mostly on weekends, over a two-week period, after which we were to read our paper aloud to the group. If the papers weren't complete enough, or seemed too superficial, I knew Shirley rejected them and they would have to be redone. I did my best to include everything the first time. My paper was twenty-five pages long, but took me three weeks to write. This extra week delayed the next step and therefore extended my treatment.

On weekdays, we spent afternoons and evenings in classes or lectures. I felt like I was back in school, but this time what I was learning would help save my life.

We studied nutrition, the disease concept of alcoholism, and its stages. I was surprised to learn that at least ten-percent of the U.S. population is alcoholic. A very small percentage make it into any kind of treatment program and only one in thirty-five of us who enter treatment stay clean and sober for the rest of our lives. The instructors told us over and over again that unless we were willing to go to any length to maintain our sobriety, we wouldn't survive.

This meant a willingness to put sobriety before family, friends, business, personal relationships, and anything else that might stand in the way. It was frightening to learn that most people don't make it and that practicing alcoholics end up in jails, mental institutions, or die drunk. The only way to avoid one of these fates is to stay in recovery. I believed them, and I thank God I did. For some of the patients, the unrelenting withdrawal, demanding regimen, and lack of freedom was just too hard, and they dropped out or were told to leave. It was difficult for me, too, but my desire to live and get well overcame my discomfort and feelings of rebellion.

The nights continued to be the most difficult. I still held on to the idea of calling the boys to have them come get me, and rehearsing what I would tell them if I did. But as morning came, the daylight and smiling people reminded me that I, too, could get better, and I started through another day.

Some days, one of the kids would visit. Patti was busy with her new baby, three hundred fifty miles away in Bellingham, but the others stopped by often. Jim, Fred, and David were there regularly and Lois Jane came from Alaska, staying at the house so she could be close. Lissie was living with a family in Jefferson and concentrating on getting her credits for graduation. Some dear friends of Jim's and mine brought her to visit. I was relieved to see her again and know that she was okay. I couldn't believe how warm and loving she was to me.

After two weeks I was still having feelings of hopelessness and my endurance was running out. I anguished over my discomfort and about continuing, but then I called Patti, the only one of my children I hadn't talked to yet, and she encouraged me to stay with the treatment. Her words and loving attitude helped. This was a turning point for me. I now knew that all six of my children were behind me. None of them had abandoned me. I never again felt so helpless and desperate that I wanted to be put away in a place where I could just be medicated and out of my misery without going through this torment.

The symptoms of withdrawal changed over the first few weeks, and were especially intense because I was withdrawing from both alcohol and prescription drugs. I couldn't stand in one place without holding on to something because I would become dizzy and lose my balance. Any exertion made me short of breath and weak. By now, my legs had swelled to the size of stove pipes and had no feeling. I still couldn't focus my eyes well and had trouble retaining what I read in class. There was a constant buzzing in my ears and I was continually fighting feelings of disorientation.

Eventually, once or twice a day, brief waves of relief washed over me. They lasted, at most, a few minutes. This would go on for months. Over time, the waves lasted longer and I learned that I could sometimes trigger them with a bath or shower, simple exercises, or a short walk. These feelings gave me hope and at the same time made me desperate to get even more relief.

With at least thirty patients in treatment at one time, we had a thirty-day sobriety celebration almost daily. Everyone came, including the kitchen help. We acknowledged individual accomplishments with tears and hugs when people were awarded their medallions. Then they left us.

As one sober person would leave, another drunk or drugged one would arrive. Each newcomer would slip into withdrawal and fear, just as I had, and before long I found myself feeling a responsibility to reach out to them. Sometimes I was able to offer comfort to new people coming in. This made me feel even stronger. But, I had to accept that not everyone could be helped.

One day, after lunch had been served and nearly everyone had eaten and left, I had a frightening experience. I was relaxing at a table near the window and enjoying one last cigarette before returning to class. John, a patient, casually walked into the courtyard and as he kneeled down in front of the window I saw he had a knife in his hand. He slowly and deliberately raised the knife and inserted it into his stomach. I screamed and the kitchen staff appeared quickly. There was a great hustle with getting towels to sop up blood. The nursing staff arrived to attend him, and an ambulance came to whisk him away. John lived, but was put in the psych ward. I never saw him again. He hadn't been able to cope with the withdrawal and had managed to get the knife out of the kitchen without being seen.

As for me, there was always someone there to offer encouragement. They continually reminded me of how long it had been since I had had that last drink, and how much better life would be as time went by.

One basic tenet of recovery was the need to connect with God or some Power greater than self. This was a difficult concept for me to accept, because, again, I felt so unworthy of God's grace. I struggled with this. I knew that I couldn't rely totally on my own willpower to stay sober, and because I didn't feel that I could turn to God, I turned to other people in recovery. I was told that they could provide that Power and that I must listen to them. They would give me the direction I needed. I found it easy to bond and get close to the other alcoholics in treatment with me.

Because I was not keeping up with the program, physically or emotionally, Shirley recommended I extend my stay an additional two weeks. Recovery was painful, even in treatment. By now, I knew how much help I needed. I was happy to stay.

The fourth week of my recovery was referred to as family week. They all six came, every day, for five days. It was then that I began to learn just how deeply my alcoholism had affected them. They all attended my group sessions as well as private sessions for the family.

At our family sessions, the children formed a circle with me in the center and each came forward, one at a time, to sit facing me. One of the worst experiences of my life was looking into their eyes for the first time in such a long time and seeing the pain and suffering I had caused. The resentments came out, too, and I felt estranged and distant from them afterward. They each told me how they felt about my drinking and how it had affected them. It must have been horrible for them as well.

According to treatment center policy, I was free to go home on a weekend pass after family week. I went, but was alone, withdrawn, and totally miserable most of the time. My children had simply told the truth, but I felt angry and betrayed. I was relieved to be back in treatment where I could share this latest pain.

The basic purpose of treatment was to get clean and sober and to stay that way. But another was to clean up my past. This meant I had to face the hurt I caused, hear it, pay attention, and then make amends. Making amends is more than saying I am sorry. The physical symptoms from the damage I had done to my central nervous system would continue for not only weeks and months, but years. It would also take years to acquire the emotional and physical ability to cope with the hurts I had caused.

One of the most painful things in my life was how my Lissie was treated as a result of my alcoholism. My most valuable amends to Lissie and to all of my family would be to live a clean and sober life. This would give me a chance to be a caring, loving, concerned parent again. And for that chance I was grateful.

Six weeks of treatment finally came to a close and I received my medallion with hugs and words of encouragement. I was expected to go home, but I was afraid to do so. I just wasn't ready to leave. I moved into a motel a few blocks from the center where I stayed for an additional week. I returned to the center each day and spent most of my time there.

I had been told repeatedly that it was important to continue in a fellowship of recovery after I left. I was instructed to come back once a week to "aftercare" meetings and I did. I felt very close to Shirley and some of the other staff members and was comforted when they told me to call them at any time. I called frequently during that first year.

Chapter 18

I was afraid. I still owned the house in town, but I felt obligated to go back to the house on the hill. I was afraid to be alone and the new house was so isolated, but I forced myself.

Shirley advised me to get back to work at least four days a week and keep a regular schedule. I had to push myself to do it. Business was bad because of the early eighties' recession. We were trying to keep four restaurants afloat. It would have been a hard time even if I had been feeling better. But I felt horrible. Any noise: a loud voice, a door closing, or the phone ringing, sent a sudden severe shock through my body. I had no stamina, and I had trouble coping with any controversy. I was jumpy and on edge about everything, and was subject to sudden outbursts of tears, withdrawal or depression. Sometimes I had to get up and leave, just to survive.

I read every book and article I could find about alcohol and drug recovery. It was helpful to know others had experienced withdrawal symptoms long into their recovery, too. It gave me hope that one day I would have my memory, nerves, and emotions restored to normal. I knew I needed to continue the daily walks I had begun at Serenity Lane. It took a tremendous amount of energy to force myself to get out the door for a couple of laps around my circular driveway, but I did it most of the time.

I pushed and stretched myself, physically and mentally, at every opportunity because I wanted to get well. To cope with the feeling of withdrawal, I exercised, ate pounds of M & M candies, read several meditation books over and over again, took hot showers, called others in recovery, and often talked to Shirley. Sometimes a brisk walk provided relief, if only temporary. When I felt that I couldn't go on, in desperation I got down on my knees and prayed. In the back of my mind, always, was the knowledge that alcohol or drugs could bring immediate comfort. Remembering how I had been just before treatment kept me from taking that first drink.

Sandy Palmer's home became a haven when I felt lonely. I often camped out in her kitchen for hours on end and watched her and her family carry on their daily life. She understood; at least she never asked me to leave. Sometimes company would drop in or she would even go away for short periods and leave me sitting. I felt safe with Sandy and not so frightened as I would have been at home alone.

In August, I reluctantly attended my first Albany fellowship meeting for recovering alcoholics. I did so with apprehension and shame. The only reason I went was because it had been drilled into me in treatment that I must do this if I wanted to stay sober.

I had also been told that I must find a sponsor, a woman with more sobriety than I, who would act as my guide and mentor. Finally, in October, I asked a woman from the fellowship if she would sponsor me. I was shocked at the condition she put on accepting me as a sponsee. She told me I must attend no fewer than four or five meetings per week! In my disbelief, I replied that she certainly meant per month. She firmly assured me that "per week" was exactly what she meant. I admired her drive and determination and I felt confidence in her. I agreed to her condition.

I also needed to reconnect with the people in my life whom I had neglected and make amends where necessary. I contacted our Episcopal priest. Father Bryce, who had replaced Father Joe, listened while I told him about my disease. I expressed appreciation for church and soon began to support the church financially again. However, I felt too unworthy to attend.

While I had talked to my friend, Don Brudvig, when I was in treatment, I had hidden my alcoholism from the rest of the Future Savings and Loan board members. They were surprised when I returned and told them what had happened and where I had been for the past couple of months. I thanked them for covering the board meetings I had missed.

Sober again, I was now able to reconnect with Mom and Daddy, at least by phone. The family had sheltered them and they hadn't known about my drinking. When I finally called, Mom didn't question why I had dropped out of their lives, but she was happy to hear from me. By this time Daddy was too senile to know whether I had called or not.

I also enjoyed getting reacquainted with my granddaughters, Courtney and Heather, when they spent a few days with me. I was much more aware of them and who they were than when I had seen them last. I was pleased to see that Heather was developing into a strong, optimistic, and joyful child. Courtney remained more delicate and reserved. We talked about the train trip we had taken a few months earlier, and I was very open with them about my alcoholism, and why I had behaved as I had. I drove them home to Bellingham, and although I needed to stop every hour for a break, I enjoyed the feeling of accomplishment it gave me.

Later that summer, I flew to San Francisco to visit David. David was doing his internship with the Marriott Company in Burlingame, California. He met me in the city for a few days and we stayed at the St.

Francis Hotel. It was great to be with him and not have to drink. That fall, I helped organize the Serenity Lane Alumni Association and served as president one year. The monthly meetings were held at my home the first two years.

In October, we celebrated Mom's eightieth birthday at brother Fred and his wife Esther's home in Ten Mile. They held an open house for friends and family and we had a beautiful time. Aunt Essie's son, Dale, was there and I was elated to see him. Dale had built a successful construction business in Bellingham, had a wonderful wife and great kids. He was six months older than I and we had been very close as children. While we had made a point to keep in contact as young adults, eventually Dale began to drink heavily and made excuses not to see me. It had been several years since we'd been together and I was so excited to see him. He had just been released from the hospital after another life-threatening crisis due to his alcoholism. I didn't get to tell him about my recovery, but was filled with hope for him. He died less than a month later when his liver gave out. I felt sick that he hadn't made it and that we wouldn't be able to share recovery.

For Christmas that year, Bunny sent me a beautiful cross-stitched and framed "Serenity Prayer." I was overwhelmed with emotion when I opened the package and read it. It made me realize that she understood how important this prayer was to my recovery.

**"God, grant me the serenity to accept the things
I cannot change, the courage to change the things
I can, and the wisdom to know the difference."**

The foggy, buzzy, cobwebby feeling in my head lingered. Over time, the periods of contentment and peace increased. In the meantime, our restaurants continued to suffer serious losses. Fred felt I still wasn't contributing much to the business. Though I was more productive than before, he said I still brought too much conflict and turmoil. My fears held back the growth Fred visualized and wanted for the company. I admittedly continued to have mood swings in my recovery. He no longer trusted me and insisted on total control of the business. The pressure was tremendous, and I finally signed over the control to him but felt resentful, negative and scared. These feelings revolved around my own loss, but I had other concerns as well. I knew Jimmy wanted to have his own Izzy's franchise someday and I hoped David would return and want to do the same thing. Now I worried that it would be harder for me to help them.

The realization that I had lost my credibility with the family hurt me to the core, but treatment had rekindled my hope. Now God was giving me another chance. I was no longer president of the corporation, nor did I hold voting stock, but after considerable thought and prayer, I decided God wanted me to focus on being supportive of my children's endeavors. Grateful for my capacity for spiritual, mental and physical growth, I considered my recovery and rebirth a gift from God. I shifted my energies to helping my children, including Fred, instead of resenting and regretting my losses.

Fred encouraged me to continue working. Although I was under no obligation to do so I was happy to contribute, and worked full-time. Now that the new structure protected Fred from my emotional ups and downs, he was able to draw on my experience, and seemed appreciative of my help. We were a team again.

By January, with restaurant sales continuing to slip, we needed to do something quickly. Fred and I toured Seattle restaurants to seek fresh ideas. We discovered the luncheon buffet concept and decided to use it. I developed new products at home and Patti and I reworked my baked bean recipe. Then we turned our attention to a special cinnamon roll Mom made at home when I was growing up. A new spaghetti recipe came next, followed by two new pizza sauces. The idea was to produce food in volume without losing the quality of small home-cooked portions. We rolled out the lunch buffet in two of the restaurants in 1982. It was well-received.

My energy level continued to increase and I continued to look outside myself even more. What a change to be able to manage more than survival again. My enthusiasm for investing in real estate returned. I bought an older house in Albany and converted it into an experimental kitchen for Izzy's. We used the living room for our managers' meetings. I made it available for other things, including an art studio for Fred's wife, Bobbie. The company paid three hundred dollars a month for the space, thereby covering my investment.

Difficult as it was to even think about, I knew it was time to visit Maggie at the nursing home. I summoned my courage. She didn't know me and I went away feeling the loss of a good friend. I could hardly comprehend the change in her. She had been so bright and alert in previous years. She died in March at ninety years old.

In June, David graduated from Oregon State with a degree in Hotel/Restaurant Management. I felt proud, but also sad when he left for Sacramento to be an assistant manager of one of Marriott's big restaurants. I flew there to visit. It was exciting to have dinner during a shift David was managing. There was my baby boy working in a position of authority for a major hotel chain. He'd grown up.

Despite my many activities and my feelings of accomplishment, there were still days I felt useless and alone. My physical and mental states were so intertwined, it was impossible for me to know where the problem originated. It was a struggle to get through those days. I began keeping a journal of my recovery, a record of feelings and hopes to be reviewed from time to time as measurement of my progress. On the hard days, I could look back at the journal and remind myself that I would also have good days. The writing began in 1982 with mostly short entries and one-liners describing the daily struggle. Here are a few:

March 8th	*Yesterday was an odd day. I felt dead inside, tense and anxious.*
March 9th	*I feel a bit down today, nothing in particular. Just felt this way when I got up.*
March 10th	*Wanted to stop and pick up M & M's on my way home today. Felt very alone. Didn't want to reach out to anyone.*
March 15th	*Terrible anxiety and fear. Withdrawn and alone. I knew I was close to the edge. Felt like screaming, crying and running. Out of the "now." Easy does it. Let go and let God. Had a restless night.*
March 20th	*Must meet life on life's terms. Accept things as they are at this moment. Stop trying to exert my will.*
March 21st	*Felt close to people today.*
March 25th	*It is too much for me. Need to let go and let God.*
March 26th	*Woke up feeling good today.*
March 28th	*I still get crazy when I don't go to meetings. I can't afford to put anything ahead of sobriety. Too dangerous.*
March 31st	*Felt blah. Wanted to be totally alone. Ended up lying down and eating a jar of peanuts. Felt full and crumby after that.*
April 3rd	*Miserable. Ate too much ice cream. Slept for an hour and still not feeling physically or mentally good.*
April 10th	*One whole week of "not good days."*
April 18th	*I thank God for this wonderful day.*

April 25th	*Seems I need to either feel hurried or a little bored. Need to work on the middle feeling.*
April 26th	*Exhausted today. Didn't go to work. Tried to sleep but can't. Laid around all day. Wish I could relax.*
April 29th	*Mom called. It was good to hear her voice.*
May 5th	*Had a wonderful weekend.*

A constant thread throughout the journal was one of feeling incomplete and alone. I was fearful much of the time and lacked confidence. On May 21st, I celebrated my first year of sobriety. By this time I not only had a sponsor, but also a sponsee. I invited them, Sandy Palmer, and three women from treatment to dinner at a restaurant in Albany. The boys and Lis Ann joined us later at a fellowship meeting where there was a celebratory cake waiting for me.

I was excited to have reached this milestone, but knew that I was still struggling to stay on this path. My feelings of unworthiness continued to plague me.

Then, one day I reviewed my entries and was amazed to find I had had seventeen "good days" in a row. Something was happening. Even so, I was impatient for more.

A part of me remained raw and alone since Jim's death. I so wanted someone to fill that void. Yet an inner voice repeatedly told me I should never again enter into a lifetime commitment. Still, I often fantasized about someone taking care of me and somehow "fixing" me. Then I met a man who was also in recovery. He took attention away from myself. This gave me some relief. Focusing on his defects rather than my own was a respite I hadn't expected. Our involvement stemmed from the rawness of recovery and an unfulfilled, ever-present longing in both of our lives.

I was up front with my concerns for the relationship. Our commitment would be limited. It would extend from one day to the next, as long as there was no friction or turmoil. It wasn't realistic, but I was as honest about my needs as I could be. We were married with this understanding seventeen months after I had finished treatment. He had twenty-two months of sobriety. Our common bond was alcoholism. We separated four months later and he moved to an apartment, but we continued to cling to each other at times. Neither of us had dropped out of recovery, but we found it more difficult to do together. We divorced after eighteen months. The turmoil eased, but I was still lonely.

I continued my daily routine of meditation, prayer, diet, exercise, and work. I was impatient, wanting the recovery process to accelerate. I had learned a man's presence in my life wasn't the answer, and I

Izzy, 1983.

attempted to fill the void with other things. There was God, the family, and many friends to occupy my thoughts. I now had three sponsees: Patty, Kathleen, and Rhoda. They helped me shift my focus away from myself.

One day, Lois Jane called from Alaska. She worked for a lumber company in Wasilla and was excited about qualifying for a low-interest loan the State of Alaska was offering to residents interested in developing the land. Real estate was a natural interest for me and I gladly loaned her five thousand dollars for the down payment. She cleared the land herself and had a great little house built. I was pleased and proud of her ambition and happy that I could help.

In July of 1983, Daddy was hospitalized with pneumonia, shortly after his ninetieth birthday. Mentally, he had been failing for several years. Over the course of the last ten years, he had had what was probably a series of small strokes. No one ever knew for sure, but we could all see that his mind was steadily deteriorating. When it finally hit me, that he was truly gone from me mentally, I was sick with grief. I denied the reality and struggled with him, trying to get him to respond to me in a normal way. Finally, I let go and accepted him as he was; grateful that he was still loving and able to take care of himself physically with guidance from Mom. Now his physical health was declining, too. When it was time to leave the hospital, he couldn't walk. We encouraged Mom to transfer him to a nursing home. I sat with him for the last time before I left for Albany. He was still in the hospital and for his safety he was tied to the bed. He begged me to take him home.

"Izzy, untie me, Baby, and I'll take you down the road to look at a horse."

This had been my treat as a child for helping with some project. Now he was calling me "Izzy" and "Baby." It felt good. I hadn't heard him call me either of those names for years. I held his hand while he fell into a deep sleep. The tears ran down my cheeks as I realized how tired his old body was.

"Please God," I prayed, "let him die with dignity."

I returned to Albany and Mom called a few days later to tell me he was gone. He died of heart failure, but with dignity, and I was grateful.

At Daddy's funeral, my cousin Erna approached me with compassion evident on her face and I held out my arms to her. We had not been friendly since she married Al thirty years earlier. She had been divorced from him now for some time, and I knew it had been painful for her and their three children. We hugged each other and she asked me to come to her home the next day for a special gathering of the cousins. After thirty years of separation, it was a great relief to be with all of them again. Aunt Irene and all four of her daughters were there as well as Mom, my sisters, and I. We made plans to hold the first "Muenscher Reunion" in July of the following year. Everyone from both "Houses" would be invited. The tears we shed that memorable day were tears of both loss and joy. I had lost Daddy, but had regained my cousins and Aunt Irene.

That same summer, I almost experienced what would have been a shattering loss. Patti's daughter, two-year-old Ashley, fell critically ill with spinal meningitis. I traveled almost non-stop to the hospital in Bellingham. Frank, Patti's husband, was in Eastern Oregon on a camping trip and couldn't be reached immediately. Ashley was in a coma for days. Patti stayed by her side continuously, stroking her and speaking to her in a soothing voice. Finally, miraculously, Ashley recovered. We were emotionally drained, but the experience had brought us closer. I saw the love Patti had for her baby, and somehow I loved her and Ashley more for what they had gone through.

In September, my granddaughter Carrie, Fred and Bobbie's second child, was born by Caesarean section. I was at the hospital for her birth. What a contrast between waiting for this baby's arrival and the wait for her older brother, Dean, two-and-a-half years before. She was dark-complexioned, beautiful like my mom, and healthy. I was so glad to be fully there.

As I began to feel better physically, I decided to take tennis lessons. I often played with my friend Linda. I complained to her if her ball didn't come straight to me because it meant I would have to run after it. I was still smoking and these short attempts at running were painful and left my heart pounding. She continued to hit the ball all over the court and I continued to run after it and complain. Nevertheless, I enjoyed the game. I felt good about being able to meet the mental and physical challenges tennis offered.

I also began to take on more responsibility with Future Savings and Loan. Interest rates were extremely high and we were in a recession, yet inflation seemed out of control. It was next to impossible to find borrowers in Albany or even in the state of Oregon. However, there were development opportunities in Colorado and California and we became involved.

Even with all that was going on in my life, I awoke each morning knowing that recovery must be my main focus for the day.

To learn more about alcoholism, Patti and I had attended a seminar on alcohol and drug intervention at Western Washington College in the fall of 1982. I also attended an all-day seminar at the state offices in Salem in 1983. I did everything I had been taught that I needed to do to continue my recovery. I knew I was making progress, but sometimes I still felt frighteningly close to the edge. I never knew what would trigger a feeling of panic. It might be checking into a motel and finding a liquor cabinet in the room, or going to a restaurant and having the server ask me what I would like to drink. I had to remind myself that "drink" didn't necessarily mean alcohol. Sometimes the panic would take me totally by surprise. Other times I could see it coming. I was usually able to overcome it, but there were times when I just didn't have the answers.

When Mom called the spring after Daddy's death to say she was coming for a visit, I was terrified. Because of Daddy's progressing senility Mom and Daddy had not been down to visit since Jim's funeral five years earlier. Now, Mom would be free to visit whenever she wanted. I was frozen at the prospect. I was sure I wouldn't be able to cope with her presence during this still vulnerable phase of my recovery. How could I protect her from the truth with her there in my own home? It seemed impossible to share my recovery with her, now. I'd worked so hard to hide even my drinking from her over the years. I trembled with fear and anxiety when I thought about her visit. Mom said she was bringing Ashley with her. I looked forward to having three-year-old Ashley, who was as bright, composed, and capable as Patti had been at that age, but dreaded the thought of spending time alone with Mom. I was afraid she would find out about my alcoholism, or that she would see how nervous, anxious, and out-of-control I was.

Bunny still didn't want me to tell Mom what had happened. She was adamant because she worried about Mom being shocked and hurt. I shared my confusion and fear with my sponsor. I gave her my plan for how I would handle it. "After all," I said, "it will be only for a few days. I can keep myself under control and I won't needlessly concern Mom with the truth about her daughter."

My sponsor responded with, "It won't work, Izzy. It is in direct conflict with your recovery. It is time you share honestly with your mother. It's time you let her know you."

Mom and three-year-old Ashley arrived at the train depot in Albany. They were quite a pair. Great-grandma and Ashley, each with carrying case in hand.

Within hours, I sat down with Mom, who had never had a drink in her life, and told her first that I drank, and then about my alcoholism. Then I told her about treatment and my sobriety. She listened intently while her small frame began to shake and tears streamed down her cheeks. She said, "Oh, honey, I am so sorry and I am so sorry you couldn't tell me. How can I help you if I don't know?" We held each other and cried together. It was the beginning of a feeling of closeness to my mother I had never before experienced. I am so grateful I was sober the last years of her life. Otherwise, I would have missed it all.

Chapter 19

In early April, 1984, I received a letter from Lis Ann who was in the Army, stationed in Germany, near Frankfurt. I was shocked to read that she was pregnant and that the baby was due in about three weeks. She had been afraid to tell me. Lissie intended to keep her baby. After a few moments of feeling the intense shock, I quickly obtained a passport and made reservations for Germany. The idea of a trip overseas was paralyzing to me. I was afraid that I didn't have the coping skills I would need in a foreign country. I also was frightened by the idea of not having my support group as a safety net. I went because it was the only way I knew to let Lis Ann know how much I loved her.

The challenge began shortly after take-off from New York. The alcohol poured freely and created the feeling of a night club. I didn't want to be in that environment, with the temptation of alcohol being offered to me. I sat rigidly throughout the long flight trying desperately to focus my thoughts elsewhere.

My troubles continued when I arrived in Germany. I had no idea there would be several hospitals in the area or that I would have so much difficulty communicating.

I couldn't find Lis Ann.

After a day-and-a-half of calling from my hotel, trying to make myself understood, I finally spoke to someone in a maternity ward who recognized Lis Ann's name and connected me to her room. I was so relieved to hear Lis Ann's voice on the other end. She was surprised and thrilled that I was there. I got a taxi and went immediately to the hospital where I saw my blond, blue-eyed grandson, Eryc James Covalt.

I stayed in Germany until after Lis Ann and Eryc were released from the hospital. While I was there, I wrote daily in my journal, and used this writing to reflect on my relationship with Lissie and on how hard much of her life had been.

Journal entry, Tuesday, May 8, 1984
I have lots of good feelings about Lis. She right now is not only able to take care of herself—by that I mean clothe and feed plus

emotionally—but she seems capable of providing all that Eryc needs, too. Not many twenty-one-year-old women are that capable. She is not dependent on any one person and for that I am grateful. Bless her heart. I do love her very much. I hope I can tell her today how I feel about her and that I know the tough times she had had. In 1973 she was only ten years old: I was sick. In 1975, David was sick. In 1976 she was thirteen: her dad was sick. In 1978 she was fifteen: her dad died. In 1979 she was sixteen: her mother was in the beginnings of a lawsuit and terribly obsessed with self.

In 1980 she was seventeen: mother in lawsuit, mother obsessed with drinking. In 1981: mother going to bottom with alcoholism, Lis seventeen, almost eighteen. Me totally obsessed with alcohol. Kicked Lis out of house at eighteen: she was on her own from then until now.

I drew on her from age ten, more than anyone knows except maybe her. She was the light of my day when I was sick, always willing to give of herself to me. Taking care of my personal needs that I couldn't ask anyone else to do at times. I never feared what she would expect in return. You see there was about a month in 1973 and another month in 1975 when I was bedridden, unable to take care of my own physical needs. Jim probably knew how much I needed her. I am sure no one else did. The important thing is I guess that she never showed me anything but love and caring.

I shared my writing with Lissie and we cried together. Seeing Lissie go through another crisis in her life, the old pain of how I hurt her because of my drinking haunted me yet again. I was scared and tense most of the time I was in Germany, but glad I had come. I think Lis Ann got my message: "I love you."

Back home, I pushed myself daily, sometimes close to the edge. I was still recording how I felt in my journal. I had my code system: good, pretty good, difficult, and very difficult. It was encouraging to see more good days in a row. I was also diligently charting my walking progress. By now I was walking one to two miles daily and was still playing tennis regularly.

In early spring of 1984, Lois called from Alaska and sounded happier than I'd heard her in a while. She told me about Paul, that she was in love and planned to be married in mid-July. She wanted the whole family to attend. Patti and I helped her with a budget and plans. Everyone except Lis and Eryc, who were in Germany, flew to Alaska to attend the wedding. There were thirteen in all. Even Mom went.

Lois was still living in Wasilla, about forty miles north of Anchorage. She and Paul planned to make their home in the beautiful little house she had built. We stayed in a nice resort in Wasilla. The wedding was held at a horse ranch nearby. Dean and Ashley were ring bearer and flower girl and Courtney and Heather were also part of the ceremony. Lois Jane was beautiful and rode on horseback to the ceremony and again for the recessional, with Paul walking beside her. I had mixed feelings about this marriage; I felt Lois was giving up her independence for this man whom I didn't know well. I later learned to trust and respect Paul, and to love him.

About this time, to my delight, Jim and David began to talk seriously about owning an Izzy's franchise together. We discussed ways in which I could help them get started. We formed a corporation, "Covalt Brothers, Inc.," to run the business. Because I supplied all the capital, I held ninety percent of the stock and they each held five percent. This structure allowed me to get the necessary tax write-off and lower the risk for all of us. We drew up an agreement for them to purchase my stock for a nominal amount as soon as they reached certain bench marks. As a separate venture, I would buy the property and build the restaurant, leasing it back to Covalt Bros., Inc.. Jim and David would own the franchise.

Eventually, we found a piece of property in Gresham. Buying the property and building the restaurant was a big stretch for me financially. I borrowed the money at fifteen percent. Even though I was making payments of over $7,000.00 per month, I knew I was making very little headway on the principal at this high interest rate. My only hope for ever paying the loan off in my lifetime was for interest rates to drop and for me to refinance.

While the Gresham restaurant was under construction, I continued to work full-time with Fred. By now we had five company restaurants and two franchises. The five company restaurants, Albany, Corvallis, Bend, Eugene, and Springfield, were doing better than they had for a couple years. The McMinnville franchise was showing signs of success, but the Vancouver franchise was struggling. Sales in the Vancouver restaurant were very low and franchisees Al and Pam worked long hard hours without much promise of success. The survival of the Vancouver Izzy's can be greatly attributed to their tenacity and endurance.

In January of 1985, we held our first marketing meeting in a condo living room at Sunriver. Present were the three franchise groups: the Fortiers, Al and Pam, from Vancouver; the Amundsons of McMinnville; and Jim and David, who were now close to opening Gresham. Our one district manager, Ray Chesley, and Fred and his wife, Bobbie, were also there. We had already established that each restaurant would contribute a percentage of sales to the marketing budget. We spent two or three days calculating sales projections to derive what our marketing budget would be and discussing the details of our marketing plan.

At the marketing meeting, Fred told me he had been attending a non-smoking clinic in Corvallis and was making plans to stop smoking. He talked about the coughing and respiratory infections he struggled with. At midnight he would have his last cigarette. The next day back at the office, Fred was not smoking, but he was shivering and shaking from nicotine withdrawal. I went home upset and concerned about Fred's discomfort. David was at the house and I said, "David, I can hardly stand to work tomorrow and be around Fred and his cigarette withdrawal. I feel terrible smoking and knowing he can't." David replied, "Well, you don't have to smoke, you know."

I thought about his statement. I also thought about the dangerous effects I knew smoking had on my health. I had been walking regularly since I got out of treatment and had increased both the distance and the frequency quite a bit. But I had been reminded by sons Jim and David, who were non-smokers, that they didn't believe I could make progress in my lung expansion as long as I smoked. At best I would be breaking even. I also thought about how humiliating it would be if I were to have an illness related to smoking, and my kids again would be called upon to deal with the consequences of another addiction of mine.

The next morning I went outside and strolled toward the woods, praying to God for the strength to stop smoking. I walked back into the house feeling peaceful and free of the need to smoke. At least for that moment. When I saw Fred at work, I told him that I hadn't had a cigarette yet that morning.

He and I spent most of our waking hours together for the next several days as we went through withdrawal. He shared his non-smoking program with me, his literature and all the techniques he was trying. By the grace of God, I haven't had a cigarette since, nor has Fred.

The Gresham restaurant opened in February of 1985. I put more of myself, more money, and more risk into this new opening than anything I had done since the Albany restaurant opening in 1959. The highest sales we could hope for starting out would be about $50,000 a month; the break-even point would be around $55,000. The Portland market was new to us, and even though I had confidence in my sons, I planned to be at the restaurant almost constantly for awhile. I worked the restaurant with Jim and David and gave them feedback. We kept close tabs on the sales and the cost of sales. From the start, we tracked the cash flow closely. I had additional back-up cash earmarked to loan the corporation for the operating losses which I anticipated. That cash was never needed. This was the first time I had seen a positive cash flow so soon after opening since that first restaurant in Albany. Our first month's sales were $55,000 and sales never dropped below that.

That restaurant showed me what could be done if the customer's expectations are not only met, but exceeded. It is not always possible to operate this way, but our goal was to have every customer leave, wanting to come back. I believe the boys did a great job of this. In addition to careful management and treating the customers well, much of the success of the Gresham restaurant had to do with the quality of the food they served. They placed a special emphasis on freshness, abundance, and presentation, and were careful that hot food was served hot and cold food was served cold. People not only came back, but also talked about us in a positive way. Word-of-mouth really does work.

Soon after the restaurant opened, I decided to focus particular attention on the salad bar. I worked on enhancing the presentation and, in my home kitchen, I experimented with new products. I developed the chocolate cream mousse, the raspberry cheesecake, and several pasta salads.

We established gourmet salad day in Gresham every Thursday. I made the salad and desserts in my home, loaded them in my car and drove the eighty miles to the restaurant where I hostessed and helped with presentation and maintenance of the salad bar from about 11:30 to 1:30.

Because the Springfield restaurant was still new and very low in sales, I began to do the same thing there every Friday. Before long, we added a gourmet salad day in Eugene, Albany, and Corvallis. I worked closely with the managers in each restaurant. We went over the details of fruit and produce selection, purchasing, and display. I also devised a system to train salad bar employees on proper icing and product rotation.

Gourmet salad day was always a Wednesday, Thursday, or Friday. I was still doing all the extra food preparation and delivery out of my home, but I could no longer do it by myself. I convinced Marilyn Lambert, my part-time three-hour-a-week cleaning woman, to stop doing my house and yard work, and to help me with food preparation and shopping. Her daughter helped me with delivery.

Every Wednesday I worked at the Albany and Corvallis restaurants, dividing my time between the two locations. On Thursday, I continued to go to Gresham and stayed the whole day. On Fridays, I worked the Eugene and Springfield restaurants. The customers were so enthusiastic about our special salad days, we decided to make Wednesdays gourmet salad day in all eight of the restaurants. Marilyn and I could no longer do everything alone, and we hired a couple women to help on Tuesdays and Wednesdays. Gene Borthwick, the husband of one of the women, Evelyn Borthwick, came out of retirement to become the delivery driver and to do my yard work.

In addition to the upgraded salad bar, the company had already added the hot buffet and our pan pizza to the menu. It was time to somehow get the word out to the public. We had been doing T.V. commercials with little or no response. Fred and our former advertising agency had discussed my being in a commercial. In fact, they videotaped a test and the consensus was that it didn't come off well.

We held a second marketing meeting at the coast. The cabin we used for meetings was owned by Stan and Sharon Amundson, our McMinnville franchisees. Some of us stayed at the Amundson cabin and some of us stayed in a motel nearby. By now we had hired a new advertising agency, Petzold and Associates, from Portland and Keith Petzold attended this marketing session. Up to this point, we had not arrived at any marketing magic, but knew we needed to do something to increase our sales. Jim suggested we again try having me in a commercial. Fred picked up on it and Keith liked the idea. This was the beginning of the spokesperson T.V. commercials.

The first commercials were filmed at our Santa Clara location in Eugene in one night. We started the filming at about midnight after closing the restaurant and this gave us six or seven hours with no customers and no employees except those needed to help prepare the food shots. This was intense, hard work, but exciting and fun. Our production budget was low because we only had eight restaurants at the time. We crammed three commercials into that first night of filming. Although we could afford only sparse television placement, we were delighted by the tremendous response.

In August, Lois Jane flew down from Alaska and brought her five-week-old daughter, Katie, with her. They spent time with Patti, then came down to Oregon for a few days with me. Katie was a replica of Lois and I was thrilled to see her, hold her close, and love her. While Lois and Katie were down visiting the family, her husband, Paul, and his brother built a new place for them to live. It was forty miles North of Wasilla in the wilderness. There was no electricity and their water came from the nearby river. I was concerned about their living in such a harsh, remote spot with no telephone, no store, or other conveniences. But when her brief visit was over, Lois went happily back to Alaska to join Paul.

About this time, my sister Bunny moved back to Ten Mile. She had reluctantly retired from teaching and she and Pete sold their pizza business in Montana. Pete was anxious to get back to Whatcom County and Bunny was happy to be closer to Mom. They bought a house from my brother, Fred, right behind Hinotes Corner, which he still owned and operated.

In the fall, Bunny and I invited Mom to go to New Brunswick to visit her brother, our Uncle Leonard, who Mom rarely saw since his move from Chilliwack, British Columbia, years earlier. This was a tremendous trip for the three of us to share and we spent several pleasant days with our uncle. I realized what freedom it was for me to travel with Mom and not be concerned about alcohol or cigarettes. Those two things had stood between us for years. I felt remorse for the way I had separated myself from her, emotionally, even when we were together, and was so grateful that I could not only have these feelings of warmth and love for her, but that I could share them with her.

Son Fred at Izzy's Pizza Restaurant opening in Everett, Washington, 1989.

Izzy and daughter Patti at Everett Izzy's, 1989.

Opening of the Eastport Izzy's Pizza Restaurant, Portland, Oregon, 1989. Clockwise: Son Jim Covalt, Big Jim's niece Shannon Dahl, Margo's husband Arnie Dahl, Big Jim's sister Margo, son David Covalt, and Shannon's son, Mitchell Stine.

Soon after I returned from my trip with Mom and Bunny, I ran my first competitive race. Although I had stopped smoking at the end of January, it wasn't until June of that year that I had been able to add running to my daily workout. I had started with five-minute increments and gradually increased the amount I ran until, by November, I could go forty or fifty minutes without stopping.

My first race was a five-kilometer run in Portland. My friend Jeanette and I went up together to compete in that race. At times I felt like vomiting, but I completed the race; my time was a thirteen-and-a-half-minute mile. I felt good about the achievement of being able to run at all, and later, I even competed in a few tennis tournaments.

For Thanksgiving I went to Fayetteville, North Carolina, where Lissie was now stationed. I shared Thanksgiving dinner with her and Eryc and met Tony, who was from Puerto Rico. I liked Tony a lot, but suggested he and Lissie wait a while to be married. To my shock, they were married ten days after I left. While I would have preferred that she had waited longer before marrying Tony, I was proud of Lissie. She was doing her job, raising Eryc, and taking care of herself. I was grateful that she and I could now have a loving relationship again, and wished her and Tony the best.

I ended 1985 with good feelings about myself and was happy to see good things happening in my life and in the lives of my family. But Mom's stroke brought about a change for all of us for which we weren't prepared.

Izzy and her grandson, Dean Jansen, just finishing a race, 1989.

Chapter 20

Bunny called me in mid-July of 1986 to tell me she had gone to visit Mom and found her on the floor near her bed in a semi-coma. Mom, who at eighty-five years old, had been living on the farm by herself, driving her own car, and very much in charge of her life, was now in the hospital. Devastated, I rushed to join my brother Fred and sisters Bunny and Elinor to be with Mom.

I looked down at Mom's small body and into her black eyes and it was easy to see that the fiery brightness was no longer present. Instead there was a dullness never before there. I didn't know that from then on, I would only catch tiny glimpses of Mom as I had known her before. The stroke affected her more mentally than physically. Bunny was committed to having Mom live with Pete and her, but after a couple of months it was apparent to me that it was too stressful for them to have Mom stay permanently. I urged Bunny to move her to a nursing home. This was extremely difficult for Bunny, but with support from all of us, she did it.

Bunny, Elinor, Fred, or a grandchild went daily to be with Mom. I flew to Bellingham once a month, went directly to the nursing home and stayed for hours. It was sometimes hard to reach her, she seemed to be acting by rote, but she always came alive when I played the piano. I would play a familiar hymn or a favorite song and, as she had done when I was a girl, she joined right in. Even though her voice was no longer strong and smooth, it thrilled me to hear her sing. I encouraged others to join us. It was a warm, relaxed time for me. I always left with a feeling of fulfillment and peace.

Mom had always enjoyed eating out and Bunny or Elinor often picked her up at the nursing home and took her to lunch. After her stroke, she was never completely lucid, but she often surprised us with moments of clarity. For example, if Bunny seemed reluctant to take her out for lunch on a day Mom wanted to go, Mom, knowing that I had always enjoyed taking her out to eat more than others did, would tell Bunny, "Never mind, I'll wait until Isabel gets here." A year earlier, she would have organized a lunch with friends or with us and driven to the restaurant herself. While the stroke had made Mom childlike and sweet, and she accepted her changed situation, it made me sad that she was now so dependent.

The summer of her stroke, Mom was able to attend the Muenscher cousins' reunion. About eighty-five of us came. It was wonderful to see Mom and her dear sister, Aunt Irene, together, sometimes holding hands, surrounded by their many children and grandchildren. I was grateful that Mom's stroke had not been more severe, and that we still had her with us.

I went home for all of the many family gatherings while Mom was ill. Birthdays, holidays and all celebrations became more important than ever for me. I wanted to be there to share them with Mom and to be close to her.

Meanwhile, I continued to work on my own recovery from alcoholism. I was grateful for my successes thus far, and knew I could look forward to more.

Still, I continued to have severe feelings of emptiness and fear. The change in the stock ownership and my position in the company had left me grieving and sometimes resentful. I desperately wanted to get to the other side of those feelings. A friend attending Oregon State told me of a woman counselor on campus who was helping her with some issues. She suggested her counselor, Joyce, might meet with me privately, off campus.

I contacted Joyce and we agreed to go to Nendel's in Corvallis for lunch. I arrived early. I saw no one who resembled the person I was to meet, but I did notice a young-looking woman with waist length black hair—no make-up, and wearing a very long black coat. She, too, was strolling back and forth, back and forth. She was the only other person in the lobby where I had agreed to meet Joyce. Eventually I paused, as did she.

I said, "You're not Joyce?" and she said, "Are you Izzy?" I saw a shocked look on her face and I felt the same way she looked. We both realized we were the two meeting for lunch. She later described to me her disbelief in seeing a woman in a pink cashmere suit at Nendel's who certainly did not fit the image of the woman she thought she was going to counsel. The mutual friend who had referred me to Joyce was an earthy, financially-struggling student, and Joyce was looking for the same kind of person in me.

Joyce and I met at my house on Tuesday evening for about two years. She came directly from Oregon State University and I had dinner ready for us. We ate and then worked for about an hour. Each week I did some writing to share with her. I quickly built great trust in Joyce and was able to tell her my deepest feelings. She helped me with the guilt and pain, and with the losses I had incurred as a result of my drinking. I felt that I had lost so much. I had lost my dignity, my business, and I was afraid of a future where I was no longer needed.

One of the counseling issues we dealt with was my work. I was still involved in every aspect of the company. We had filmed more commercials and sales increases mounted in all the restaurants. Some continued as high as one hundred percent over the prior year's sales. Business was good! But that wasn't enough.

I was still feeling unfulfilled and vulnerable.

Gradually, I came to know that to overcome my pervasive fear of losing more than I already had, and to get over my resentment, I had to change my expectations. I needed to be less dependent on Covalt Enterprises for money, identity, and meaning. I had to learn to contribute to the company without expecting anything in return, nurturing it as though it were mine, even though I was painfully aware that it wasn't.

This shift in my perspective was the beginning of a new-found freedom for me. I learned that I could give without constraint; but putting this discovery into practice took time, and wasn't always easy. To ease this emotional transition, and to distract me, I decided to throw my energies in a new direction. Joyce and I discussed what attributes would be necessary for my new venture. I wanted a place where I could fulfill my need to help others help themselves. I knew, within the context of my new-found sobriety, that whatever I did had to have my own values in it, had to be part of a spiritual path. I also needed something I could again call my own. I needed something over which I had some control.

As I looked at the potential for expansion of the salad bar in the restaurants, I realized that this could be the vehicle that would allow me to meet my needs while providing a service to the company. Although I was personally subsidizing the operation and didn't have the capital to fund it indefinitely, I knew that what I was doing was meaningful. I felt I was providing women with a safe place to work, where they could feel supported and have opportunity to grow. I was committed to making it work.

As the dessert and salad usage increased and all the restaurants began serving the new products seven-days-a-week, I needed more space for preparation and storage. I wanted to keep the business at my house if at all possible. I gave serious thought to remodeling my garage into additional space or maybe turning the barn into a kitchen facility. Finally, I decided it would be best to remodel the old house I had bought years before on Fourth Street. The house needed a new foundation and a new roof. We purchased a portable freezer and had a small walk-in cooler built. I also had a studio and bath built for myself. This made it convenient for me to shower and dress after a game of tennis or a run, without the drive home.

We were able to move in and start production at what we decided to call "Izzy Covalt Kitchen" early January of 1988. This was two-and-a-half-years after the first salads were made and delivered by me to Springfield and Gresham.

By fall, with new Izzy's restaurants opening at a rapid rate, we needed more employees and even more freezer and refrigeration space.

This required additional financing and construction. Soon I moved my personal and business records to the kitchen, too. We used the converted living room as office space.

I continued to meet with Jim and David every week in Gresham. We found it too disruptive to continue our meetings at the restaurant. We rented a meeting room at a motel, broke at noon and I would go to the restaurant to do one of my favorite jobs, what I call "working the floor." By this time, the boys were doing so well they were turning people away at the door. I went in to work with the crew wherever help was needed during the busy lunch hours.

Once a year, I went to the coast or the mountains for a goal and planning session with Jim and David. We usually spent two full days at this task. We also attended the National Pizza Conventions together, Las Vegas first and then in Orlando, Florida where we also went to Disney World for a couple of days.

I remained very involved in all aspects of Covalt Enterprises. We continued to open restaurants. One opened on Lancaster in Salem, then Tualatin opened as a franchise unit. Behind that came Hillsboro, Hazel Dell in Washington, and Eugene on Franklin Blvd., all franchisees.

In 1987, we still occupied the original office/commissary on Pacific Blvd. in Albany, next to the first Shakey's building. But we had outgrown both the office and the commissary space. Fred located a larger location downtown on Lyon Street. With some minor remodeling and some new equipment in place for the commissary, we made the move. I felt heartache as I drove past the old place every day on the way to work. Memories of what I had built there, and lost, flooded in. I had fond memories of my children, hard at work at their early jobs there, and, of course, I thought of Jim and how we'd worked there together for so many years. Those days were gone. I was no longer in control, but I went to work at the new place ready to face whatever challenges awaited me.

Problems in 1987 on a corporate level included growth and planning in all areas. Fred needed more help and he knew it. He hired a consultant from Salem and in the fall of 1987 we did in-depth strategic planning. At this time, Fred was handling both operations and development. Acquisition of suitable sites took both time and a special talent, as did monitoring the construction. In January, 1988, we hired a Vice-president of Development. We decided Fred would stay with operations. We were now ready for more growth.

Meanwhile, the family was also growing. Lis had given birth to Derek on October 9, 1986. I went back to Fayetteville to see Derek and spend time with Lis and family again. Like Tony, Derek had beautiful dark olive skin and I fell in love with him on sight. Tony was so proud.

In January of 1987, another grandson, Karl, was born to Lois at their home in Alaska. She, Paul, Katie, and baby Karl, who was just hours old, traveled to Willow to a phone to share the good news with me. I was amazed that they would venture out into the dark freezing Alaska winter to make the call so soon after the baby's birth. It was another indicator of how well Lois was suited to her life in Alaska.

In 1988, Covalt Enterprises held the marketing meeting in Hawaii. Sales continued to increase, more units were built, more franchises were sold and business was flourishing. I felt we had a key to the magic of ongoing success, but I also worried that we might be getting too loose, letting go of too much control. It wasn't until later that this reality hit home. Meanwhile, though, personal events interrupted my focus on business.

The evening of March 16, 1988, son Fred called me shortly after I returned home. He said "Aunt Bunny has been trying to reach you. Grandma died."

I felt terrible physical pain. I felt that something was being torn from my body. I had never before experienced this kind of wrenching pain. It was excruciating and unbearable. I felt a surge of nausea and shaking and then I began to sob. I sobbed for hours, like never before.

Mom's death was far more painful than Daddy's had been. I felt a peace with his death. With Mom's death I could only feel shock and loss. The next morning I chose to drive to Bellingham by myself. I wanted to be alone, even though the tearing in my chest continued and I cried most of the way. As I neared Bellingham, it suddenly occurred to me that my sisters and my brother, Fred, must surely be devastated, too. It shocked me to realize that I was not accustomed to thinking of others when I was in pain, myself. It was something I wanted to work on in the future.

I made many trips that spring and summer to Bellingham. I found it soothing to be close to my roots, and to Bunny and Pete, as I healed. Bunny's responsible nature had come shining through as our parents had aged. Somehow, she helped fill the void left in my life by Mom and Daddy's death.

In the early summer of 1988 an assistant of Congressman Denny Smith's called requesting me to speak at a women's business and professional conference he was sponsoring in Portland. I was both flattered and frightened and said I would need time to think it over. Patti, Fred, Jimmy and David all encouraged me to do the speech. I agonized over it for several days. I had never made a formal public speech, and I wasn't sure I could do a good job. In fact, I had turned down speaking opportunities in the past. At last, however, I decided to go ahead with it. After preparing my speech, I reviewed it with Joyce. She reminded me that this speech was another way in which I could give to others and that I had an important message to share, one that was particularly valuable for women.

Mid-September arrived and I felt grateful and close to tears as I sat at the head table next to Denny Smith. I thought about how far down I had gone and here I was, ready to share a story of success with a room full of about two hundred women. I looked out into the crowded room and spotted my sons Jim and David in an audience otherwise comprised entirely of women. They were the only ones in that audience who knew how far down alcohol had taken me.

I was also bursting with pride. I thought about what Jimmy had said right after I left treatment, "Too bad, Mom, that you had to go 'out' the way you have. I am sorry you couldn't have stopped your business career when you were still a success and on top." I felt like I was on top again, and it felt wonderful.

I thought about Big Jim and how proud he would be of me. Denny Smith rose and introduced me. I stood up and adjusted the microphone. My heart was pounding. I felt light-headed and I was shaky, but as I moved into my life story about family and business experiences, I felt the tension easing. I spoke about my childhood, my life with Jim, and how we built our business. It was hard for me to talk about Jim's death, but I got through it. I told them that I had gone through a time of desolation and that I had reconnected to God.

When I finished, there was tremendous applause and many women approached me, some with tears in their eyes, and thanked me for sharing. It was exhilarating and lifting and it now felt right for me to have passed on some of what I had experienced and learned.

Epilogue

In the eleven years since my speech for Denny Smith, I've given many speeches to many different audiences. This is just one way I've continued to grow and share my experience, strength, and hope with others.

In 1981, at age fifty-four, when I entered treatment for my alcoholism, I did so only to survive. At that time, I had no interest in learning anything new or achieving more than I had already done. I felt that I had accomplished all that was needed of me. But in the end, I felt little peace and my only refuge was to take enough alcohol and prescription drugs for some "passout" time. This killed all of my discomfort. I felt nothing emotionally, no guilt, no ambition, and no self-doubt. Plus it gave me escape from the intolerable and continual shaking and nausea. My only goal at this point in my life was to hold on and maintain in hopes of having some little peace.

While I knew I had nothing to give others, I was trying hard not to take, either. But, of course, I was taking from my family emotionally every day. Today, more than eighteen years later, I not only take care of myself, but have enough left over, mentally, physically, and spiritually, to give some back to those I love. The memory of the damage I did to my children, and especially to Lis Ann, while I was drinking is extremely painful to me. I try not to dwell on this too much because I can't change the past. But I can focus on being a loving, caring, nurturing mother today.

Recovery, for me, is the joy and the awareness that I am again a valuable human being with a purpose for living. It is through serving God as I understand him that I believe I can attain and feel that sense of purpose in my life. I can support my family, friends, employees, and other recovering alcoholics on their individual paths. I also believe it is my duty to reach beyond those who are close to me and contribute to the community.

I am far from done with the things I want and need to do.

Izzy Covalt Kitchen continues to be an important part of my life. We make almost a ton of chocolate mousse each week, plus soups, pasta salad, wild rice pepperoni stuffing, sauces, and desserts. We've come a long way since 1985 when we prepared a hundred pounds of chocolate mousse per week in my kitchen at home.

We now have a general manager, a production manager, and three assistant managers at the kitchen. This has given me an opportunity to exercise my independence and creativity and it also allows me to focus on other things that need my attention. The kitchen is still my focal point, however, and there I receive my mail and phone calls. Even when I am out of town, I report to the kitchen almost daily. I keep them informed at all times of my comings and goings, and they keep me up-to-date on all my business happenings.

I like the feeling of integrity and service that prevails at the kitchen. Everyone gives constant care and attention to every product and to each individual restaurant. It is wonderful to be able to have so much trust and confidence in a group of people.

Our goal at the kitchen is for every person to work the number of days and hours each week that they want. We don't do overtime except in extreme need. Everyone, part-time or full-time, shares in our monthly bonus plan, in our retirement program, and they get a paid vacation. We also contribute one-half the premium to the optional medical insurance.

We are still evolving as our production changes. I have made sporadic attempts in the past five years to establish outside sales to reduce our reliance on the Izzy's chain as our only customer. With only one customer—regardless of who it is—we are simply too vulnerable. Also, I believe in our products. We add no preservatives or MSG. The home-cooked quality and flavors set us apart. Nobody else has what we offer, plus we do custom products.

Potential customers include grocery stores, institutions such as colleges or hospitals, or even door-to-door delivery. Each of these markets presents special hurdles. For example, shelf space in grocery stores is limited, and it is seemingly impossible to get new products online. There have been times when I have been discouraged with the lack of success in opening these new markets. During these times, I have serious thoughts of going through the process of closing down the kitchen, taking my recipes, which include many that have never yet been served in an Izzy's, and organizing them into a recipe book that I would offer to the public. Our current leads, though, are exciting, and I'm feeling optimistic at present.

As I had hoped, the kitchen has contributed toward fulfilling my continuing need for purpose and meaning in the business world. I don't know what the future holds for the kitchen. I do know that for it to grow under my leadership, I must continue to devote ample time and energy to it. But my interest is also being drawn elsewhere.

In the past eleven years Covalt Enterprises has grown, too. We have twenty-seven restaurants, nearly half of them franchises, and two delivery operations. Even with my diminished role in ownership and

The staff at Izzy Covalt Kitchen, 1998. Front row: Stephanie Lopez, Janna Gerig, Linda Smith, Marilyn Lambert (at mixer). Second row: Terry Vetkos, Izzy Covalt. Back row: Tina Keogh, Janet Spowehn, Sandra Ogle, Melodie Thomas, Tania Forbes, Kristin Romviel, Sherry Rogers, Gia Brown, Linda Townsend.

A planning session at Izzy Covalt Kitchen, 1998. Jan Lowen, Cheryl Schultz, Chris Engel, Izzy Covalt.

control there have been times when the rapid growth has stretched me beyond my capacity both financially and emotionally.

Our growth continued unchecked until 1993, when we went through a difficult period where we suffered some painful losses and had to make internal adjustments. This was primarily because things got out of balance. There are so many details which must work together for a restaurant to succeed. The affordable location and the ability to market effectively are musts. If you can't get people through the door, you have no chance. Once they arrive, the food must be quality and appropriately priced. The staff must be well-trained and friendly, and the atmosphere comfortable and clean. If any of these variables get out of balance, the restaurant won't make it. And that is what happened with the six Izzy's in California. We had to close them.

After a short but successful leveling-off process, Covalt Enterprises surged forward into more expansion and change. The stresses within the company and between the company and the franchisees have increased during this period. At times, this internal conflict has taken the focus away from where I feel it needs to be.

My role in all of this today is one of offering my opinion and also being present and supportive whenever and wherever it is appropriate and possible. Fred and I talk frequently, and I attend board meetings and strategic planning meetings.

My main goal is to continue to encourage a feeling of integrity, trust, and service throughout the company. To me, these factors are critical in getting this business back in balance.

Despite these internal problems, we have maintained standards with our employees and operations. When I walk into one of the restaurants, as I do frequently, the hard work and dedication of the people who work at Izzy's still come through. I am reassured and confident that our customers are being well taken care of.

The family has grown dramatically. To my delight, Jim married Jeanie Nelson in 1989, an energetic, enthusiastic young woman he met when she came to work in the Gresham restaurant.

David is also married now. He married Elizabeth Cole, a soft and beautiful young woman from Portland, and they have three children. James was born in 1990, Matthew in 1994, and Amy in 1995.

Lois has a total of six children, now. She had Jake in 1989, Jared in 1991, Korbett in 1993, and Sanna in 1995.

Lis Ann has three children. Amanda was born in 1988.

Patti is a grandmother! Her daughter Courtney is the mother of Hilary, who was born in 1992, and Lucas, born in 1996.

In all, I have seventeen grandchildren and two great-grandchildren. Each one is important to me and I want to establish and maintain a growing love and knowledge with each one of them. This

Izzy and her six children, Izzy in front. First row: Lois Jane, Lis Ann, Patti. Back row: Fred, Jim, David.

Izzy, her children, her grandchildren, and her great-grandchild, 1995. In front: Derek Pedraza, Jake Hein, Amanda Pedraza, Jared Hein, Eryc Covalt. Second row: Karl Hein, Katie Hein, Izzy Covalt, Carrie Jansen, Dean Jansen, James Covalt. Third row: Lois Jane Hein, Sanna Hein, Ashley Imhof, Courtney Imhof, Fred Jansen, Elizabeth Covalt, David Covalt, Matthew Covalt. Fourth row: Paul Hein, Korbett Hein, Patti Imhof, Hilary Imhof, Frank Imhof, Heather Imhof, Lis Ann Covalt, Jim Covalt, Jeanie Covalt.

takes time and energy and is an ongoing goal and a big challenge as well.

I take several trips a year to spend time with my daughters and their families.

Thanks to the business, I see all three of my sons frequently. And because they're nearby, I can share special occasions with their families.

I also see my brother, Fred, and sisters, Bunny and Elinor, several times a year. Bunny and Pete now own half the farm and live in our old house. I own the other half with the peat land and love to walk across it, looking out at the Canadian mountains or Mt. Baker. I think of Daddy and the peaceful times we spent there. I still rely on Bunny. I often turn to her for advice. She is like a rock to me and helps me feel connected, not only to her, but to our past.

Another important aspect of my life is my need for an intimate relationship. I have now come to believe that an intimate relationship is a God-given need in everyone. By searching for that connection with a special person, we are forced to grow as individuals and to continue on our spiritual path.

I also believe that it is only after we have become spiritually whole ourselves, and are finally able to give and receive with honesty and openness that we can attain that special connection with another person.

Some people reach this place at an early age. Big Jim was an example. By the age of twenty-three, when we were married, he was already giving me the benefit of this kind of spiritual maturity. He never wavered and I continue to cherish the unconditional love he gave me.

While I hungered to be with someone in a loving, close way after Jim's death, I wasn't spiritually ready. I became involved with men who also lacked the spiritual tools needed to sustain a vibrant, giving relationship.

I talked to Joyce, my counselor, about this in great detail as I struggled through these painful attempts. After she and I decided that our friendship was making it hard for her to be objective as my counselor, I started working with a psychologist in Salem. He helped me understand that I needed to select a man who had the same values that I did. I also came to realize that I needed to choose someone who was on a spiritual path similar to mine.

In the past few years I feel that I've made progress toward being ready to have the kind of relationship I want and need. For some, this is a lifetime struggle, and I feared that might be true of me. I feel fortunate that January of 1992, I met Vail Palmer, a man who has been supportive of me in this struggle.

Vail is brilliant, highly educated, has never smoked and never drank. He is an avid hiker, and is active in the Quaker Church to

Bunny, brother Fred, Elinor and Izzy, 1998.

which he was born. His being seems to revolve around the spiritual principles in his life, principles we share.

Even though we lived seventy miles apart, Vail became an important part of my life.

Soon after I met Vail, I began to attend the Quaker church with him, and have gone regularly since then. In 1993 I was nominated to the board of trustees for George Fox University. The university was founded by Quakers in Newberg, Oregon, over a hundred years ago. In the early days of my recovery, I would have never dreamt that I would one day be able to fill such a position. I view this commitment as one of my contributions to the community.

On January 31, 1999, seven years after we met, Vail and I were wed. My acquaintance with Vail developed first into friendship and finally into a deep and caring love which revolves around trust, respect, and a joyful feeling when we are together.

We were married in a traditional Quaker ceremony which surpassed any expectations that either of us could hope for or dream of. Almost four hundred friends and family members attended.

We are retaining an apartment in Portland, where both of us continue to be very involved, but our main residence is elsewhere.

My many and varied involvements give me a feeling of accomplishment, but I often step outside my comfort zone. I know I need to do this to grow, but I also have to be careful not to get too close to the edge.

Too much discomfort for too long could threaten my sobriety. Even though I haven't had any alcohol since May 21st, 1981, I know that I could lose everything by having just one drink.

For this reason, I continue to strive to maintain the balance I believe is so crucial to sobriety and my ability to fulfill my purpose in life. This balance can be maintained only by paying close attention to my physical, mental, and spiritual health.

By necessity, for me, physical health must come first. Six days a week I start my day with exercise, either running or walking, rain or shine. After that first five-kilometer race in 1985, I continued to run races. I averaged two to four races a year for the next ten years.

Exercise clears my mind and puts me into a meditative state. It is during my walks and runs where I am at my intuitive best. Sometimes solutions to problems that might have seemed insurmountable suddenly seem obvious to me. Exercise helps me feel creative and confident.

After exercise, I have a nutritious breakfast. I make a point of eating three good meals a day with healthy snacks in between.

I follow breakfast with a short formal meditation, prayer, and self-appraisal. The self-appraisal is sometimes uncomfortable for me, but it is a necessary part of my growth.

These steps help prepare me mentally, physically, and spiritually to begin my day.

Taking care of myself has given me more stamina and made me more efficient than I would have ever thought possible. Still, I need to rest and eat regularly to maintain a prudent reserve of self. I am careful to schedule my days so that I don't run out of energy and become unable to function.

I am fulfilled and busy, but my sobriety remains the single most important thing in my life. Without it, I know none of the things I have, or that I have accomplished, would have meaning for me. I continue to attend fellowship meetings on a regular basis and am grateful for the grace I have been granted.

The women whom I support in sobriety are a great source of strength to me and I look forward to the phone call, the sharing, and time I spend jogging or walking with them. Seeing the courage with which they face life without succumbing to alcohol or drugs is a constant reminder of the importance of the fellowship we share.

I have learned from all the experiences of my past. I have learned not only my weaknesses, but also my strengths, and can honor both.

My future looks bright and challenging. I know I will have many more opportunities for change and learning.

For all of this and more, I thank God daily.

THE END

Izzy Covalt and Vail Palmer, January 31, 1999.

Izzy's Values for Living

I must always maintain a prudent reserve of self,
and keep my life in balance by taking responsibility for my own
physical, mental, and spiritual growth.

Integrity is everything. It is the foundation of my self worth.

It is my responsibility to help build the self worth
and credibility of others.

I need to be more aware of those around me,
especially those who might require
more understanding than usual.

I must be supportive of others and willing to reach out to them
in a time of need.

I need to show that I care and show that I feel love.

I need to listen.

I also need to show support and enthusiasm at the success of others.

I need to give with no expectation of return.

In order to move forward, and to be successful,
it is essential that I trust others.

I can welcome change and be alert for new opportunities.

I need to enable the people around me
to take ownership and pride in what they contribute.

It is through serving God, as we understand him,
that I believe we can attain and feel
some sense of purpose in our lives.